WHY IS THIS HAPPENING TO ME?

WHY IS THIS HAPPENING TO ME?

DAVID EDWARDS

NEXGEN®

Building the New Generation of Believers

COOK COMMUNICATIONS MINISTRIES
Colorado Springs, Colorado • Paris, Ontario
KINGSWAY COMMUNICATIONS LTD
Eastbourne, England

NexGen® is an imprint of
Cook Communications Ministries, Colorado Springs, CO 80918
Cook Communications, Paris, Ontario
Kingsway Communications, Eastbourne, England

WHY IS THIS HAPPENING TO ME?
© 2004 by David Edwards

First Printing, 2004
Printed in the United States of America
1 2 3 4 5 6 7 8 9 10 Printing/Year 08 07 06 05 04

Unless otherwise noted, Scripture quotations are taken from the NEW AMERICAN STANDARD BIBLE®, Copyright © 1960, 1962, 1963, 1968, 1971, 1972, 1973, 1975, 1977, 1995 by The Lockman Foundation. Used by permission.

Cataloging-in-Publication Data on file with the Library of Congress

ISBN 0781441382

*To **Flipopoly**: You've lived life with a godly passion and confidence that has enabled me to see the answers to life that never fail. I'm forever grateful.*

*To **Richard and Marilyn**: The heart holds the most important commitments in life. The friendship we share rises to the top of my heart. Thanks for being my committed friends and for helping me know how to answer the questions for life.*

CONTENTS

ACKNOWLEDGMENTS

I couldn't have written this book alone. Here are some of the people who helped make it happen.

Trey Bowden: Well, I guess I won't miss a chance to say thank you for your friendship and the great partnership in ministry. Most of all, for watering the rocks in my head.

Janet Lee: You had the vision and insight to set this project in motion. You believed in the value of these books and the impact they will have on thousands of people seeking answers to the questions of life.

Trevor Bron: You took my loaves and fishes and helped multiply them beyond my wildest dreams. A single book becomes a series. Thanks for blessing my life.

Bobby McGraw: I'm still struggling to find your breaking point. Full-time student, pastor—and you still had the time and energy to transcribe this entire project. Wouldn't have happened without you. Your work has been stellar.

Jim Lynch Everybody! You're my friend, my personal doctor who kept me alive—and you drove the comedy engine so well. Better peace through science. Thanks to Eric and Jim Hawkins, for the extra comedy fuel; it helped keep the engine going.

Gary Wilde: Thank you for your surgical editing skills. You preserved the integrity of the manuscripts, communicating the truths that needed to be told, while laughing at my jokes.

Shawn Mathenia: You finally got your very own line in one of my books. *This is it.* Thank you for your friendship and for looking out for me.

Ken Baugh and Frontline: Thank you for your continued passion that shows up in your ongoing work to reach a new generation. You guys are my home away from no home.

The Sound Tracks: Train, Dave Matthews Band, Dave Koz, The Rippingtons, and Journey. Thanks for the inspiration.

The Questions for Life Series

I had just finished speaking at the White House and was eating lunch at Union Station with a young political consultant. We were halfway through our meal when I asked her, "What's life like for a postmodern inside the Beltway? You know, what kinds of questions do they ask?"

"They ask questions about the suffering and wrong in the world," she said, "about the church, and about who Jesus really is. You know, the questions that never fade."

Questions that never fade

Her label for those questions rose up inside of me, and this series of books flowed from that conversation. Postmoderns come wired with the need to answer the questions you'll find in these pages.

Most postmoderns have rejected the pat answers offered by today's spiritual leaders because they have found them to be inadequate for the daily life they face. They have seen others who accepted the ready-made answers but who still struggle making life work. They have no desire to repeat such mistakes. Instead, they challenge the real-life validity of the quick and easy answers.

The questions remain, but some of the questioners let their need for adequate answers diminish into the background. They give way to an apathy that says, "I've got more important things to do in my life than pursuing life's big questions." For others, finding resolution remains a priority. Yet even for them, life can become a never-ending "round-robin" of seeking solutions through new experiences.

Regardless of where you are at the moment, realize that the questions for life never truly fade away. They keep coming back, especially amidst your most trying times. They will keep knocking at your heart's door until you turn and acknowledge their crucial role in finding the life of your dreams. Until you take hold of real explanations, you'll remain constantly searching for the answers that never fail.

Answers that never fail

Spoken or unspoken, identified or unidentified, real answers are priceless. Until we find them, we're haunted by a lack of resolution in life. This unsettled life suffers constant turmoil and never-ending trouble. We look for direction that seems nonexistent, and this makes many of our decisions hard to live with. What price would we pay for a better way?

It's possible to spend a lifetime searching and never finding. Therefore, some would say that the reward comes not in the security of reaching the goal, but in the striving to obtain it. To these people I say: Why waste your life *looking* when you could be *living?*

The Creator of the universe holds the indelible answers we seek. They are not hidden, but they have often been obscured. They are veiled by some who place a higher value on *knowing* the answers than upon allowing the answers to change their lives. We need to push through and ask: What is the actual value of discovering answers that never fail? We'll find the value shining through in *what the answers produce in our lives*. When we discover these answers, our lives change in four supernatural ways. Finding them ...

Builds our outlook It's impossible to live a satisfying life without faith, meaning, and purpose. That's why each of us will place our faith in something or someone that is our primary value. We believe this person or thing will bring meaning and purpose to our life.

Without purpose, we'd have no reason to exist. So even the most cynical and withdrawn person seeks meaning in life. It may reside in something as mundane as keeping a pet iguana fat and happy. Or it could be that he finds meaning in something as twisted as making records and sleeping with young boys.

But life without an ultimate meaning and purpose becomes fragmented and chaotic. We roam from place to place, relationship to relationship, experience to experience, hoping to find something worth living for that endures. The iguana won't live forever. We also quickly discover that people fail us, that work is never-ending, that merely accumulating sensory experiences leads us down a continually darkening pathway.

There is no sense to life without meaning and purpose. There is no meaning and purpose without faith. And there is no faith until we answer the questions that never fade.

Brings ownership Discovering answers to the questions for life transforms us from merely being alive to actually having a life to live. We've all seen people who seem to just take up space in the world. They live for no apparent purpose. The things they do carry no meaning and make no appreciable impact on the people around them. They are alive, but they do not own a life.

The questions for life can't be glibly answered, nor should they be made impotent through intellect. They must be answered in our hearts; they must settle down into the very center of our person. Ownership of life begins when our head and our heart come together at a long-sought crossroads: where the questions that never fade meet the answers that never fail.

> 66 Ownership of life begins when our head and our heart come together at a long-sought crossroads: where the questions that never fade meet the answers that never fail. 99

Breaks us open Every question for life has a spiritual dimension. We may assume that answering the question of world hunger and suffering is only a physical matter, but that would be a wrong assumption. This question first finds its answer in a spiritual dimension, then the physical needs can be addressed in practical action. The same is true for all other questions for life; they each have a spiritual dimension.

The questions for life demand *powerful* answers that remain *present,* regardless of circumstance. The answers that never fade literally open us up to the things of God. That is, they lead us to find and apply his *power* and *presence* to the very heart of our question. These answers don't create despair; they settle disputes. They don't cause confusion; they construct a viable contract between life and us.

Brings an outworking Answering the questions for life develops an internal faith expressed in our observable behaviors. In other words, when we own the answers that never fail, our life takes on a meaning that others see and desire. This outworking of faith is extremely practical. It influences the choices we make, the words we speak, and the attitudes we reflect in daily life.

And this outworking can't help but grow a deep confidence within us. When never-failing solutions calm our internal struggles, we are able to move forward amidst seemingly insurmountable odds. We can work in an environment hostile to the things of Christ—and still live out our faith. We are confident that, although those around us may reject us, we are forever accepted by the One who matters most.

In these books, I have refused to "reheat" the old teachings. Instead of serving leftovers, I've dished up biblical answers that really do apply to the lives we live. These books keep it real, and I've written them with you in mind. I've used generous doses of humor and plenty of anecdotes (most of which actually happened to me).

I've made scant reference to other Christian authors, though, for a reason. In my attempt to make these books fresh, I chose to keep them uncluttered by the thoughts of others. Instead, I try to communicate God's thoughts from the Bible straight to your heart.

You'll notice that the title of each book forms a question. The titles of each chapter also appear as questions. But the content of each chapter *answers* that chapter's question. When read in their entirety, the chapters together answer the big question posed by each book.

You can read these books in any order; they each stand on their own in dealing with a single topic. At the end of each book you'll find questions that I hope will encourage an expanded discussion of the subject matter. Why not bring a group of friends together to talk things through?

Although this book series began over lunch inside the Beltway of Washington, D.C., I am aware that we are all bound together by the questions that never fade. As you read, I hope you will find the answers that never fail.

David Edwards
Summer, 2004

Introduction to
Why Is This Happening to Me?

"I hate God. Just look what he's done!" She sat across
from me, and her youth minister formed the third point
in our triangle of chairs. The rest of the campers had
already moved back to their cabins for bed, so we sat in
the open-air tabernacle under a security light twenty feet
overhead.

*"My mom remarried a guy who's a travel agent for
ego trips. I can't stand being in the same room with him.
And two years ago, my big brother was killed in a car
wreck on the way home from college; he was my best
friend. To top it all off, everybody in the youth group
hates me. It's not fair! Obviously, I'm not even that
important to God. I hate him!"*

•••

One of the most potent subjects discussed among
Christians today is God's role amidst suffering and evil. In
our pain, we often ask, "God, where are you?" and "How can
God be good and allow all this agony in my life?" Everywhere
I go people ask me, "Why do bad things happen to good peo-
ple ... and what is God *doing* about it?"

Most of the answers we get from church make perfect
sense, if we're sitting on padded pews and looking through

stained-glass as the organ plays softly. But once we take those answers outside into our real world, they don't seem to work. Every day we face a world filled with torment, suffering, injustice, and illness.

We need to hear something different. We need something that makes sense out of the everyday life we call reality. Otherwise, we have no options other than the ones that have already moved us onto the pathways of despair, apathy, and anger.

The church is the depot for God's truth in this world. The church has the answers the world seeks. So how is it possible that the church could be so good at concealing the truth? Better still, how do we get at the truth and apply it to our lives? We have three choices to make:

Shake off the bull

Think about the five flimsy lines we most often use as our "default setting" when facing suffering and evil. These phrases, however, are about as effective as steering the Titanic against an iceberg for a more pleasant voyage. They keep us afloat for only short distances before giving us up to the cold waters of despair. Here they are—

Pious: "It's God's will" Little Orphan Annie would put it like this: "The sun will come out tomorrow." Another way of saying it: "Think positive" or "Think happy thoughts."

Naïve: "Have you prayed about it?" This line implies that God is not able, not powerful enough, or just doesn't care what we have to face—unless we really get on his case through prayer.

Glib: "It's for your own good" We've all heard that everything contributes to a greater good. After all, God is just trying to teach us a lesson, right?

Silly: "The devil made me do it" Yes, this line used to get lots of laughs when 1970s comedian Flip Wilson used it over and over again as a repeating gag. Of course, it's still a silly way to look at life.

Tidy: "It's all under his control" How many times have you heard this one? Does it make you feel better? (To make it worse, your erstwhile comforter may also tack on: "You just need more faith.")

Spread the blame

Before we attach all the blame for evil and suffering on God, we need to recognize that there are plenty of other places it could be assigned. The fragility of life, for instance. As our bodies age, we'll spend almost anything to maintain a youthful appearance. I know some people who have more layers of plastic on their face than any three George Lucas alien characters combined.

Then there's the power of choice and the effects of our poor decisions. All of us have been given the power to choose our actions. We can choose to do evil or good, and what we choose can certainly cause us pain.

I think about how our society fixates on fast—fast food

and drink, fast cars, and fast-acting drugs. For years, people abuse their bodies and then blame God when they get sick and he doesn't heal them. Other people build multi-million dollar homes on Malibu Beach. Then, when their house is destroyed, they use a storm to justify their anger toward God. They even have the nerve to call it an "act of God." (Hey, God didn't build your condo on the beach.)

Stand on the basics

We live in a real world where the consequences of suffering are undeniable. Therefore, real people get hurt. Authentic Christianity embraces this truth and provides answers for anyone seeking the truth about his suffering.

The corollary to the truth of hurting people is this: God is always against evil. By its definition, evil is that which resists God. Whether or not we see it, God is, and always has been, doing something about evil. Evil does not have free reign over the world and our lives. It always faces its toughest opponent in the form of God.

The best way to understand the basics, then, is to examine the life of Christ while he was on the earth. While he was God on earth, he demonstrated the heart of God toward us and showed us how God deals with evil. The things Jesus believed about the suffering of all mankind, how he responded to our hurting—and what motivated him—is the focus of this book.

•••

We occupied that triangle of chairs for more than twenty minutes as the girl poured out her anger toward God. When she finished venting, I said, "I can't solve the problems in your life, but I can offer one piece of advice: You've got to stop blaming God." She looked up from the splatter marks her tears had made on the concrete, and our eyes met. "If you blame God for everything you think is bad about your life, what other source of help do you have?" I asked. "If God is removed from the equation, so is any hope for things getting better."

She stopped crying almost at once and squinted up at me. Her youth minister gave a slight nod, lending his agreement as a silent "Amen." I offered her an overview of the way Jesus dealt with evil, suffering, and pain in life. I told her how he had come to do much more than simply provide eternal life; how he had come to give us real victory over evil, along with confidence in the midst of suffering. "Jesus came to show us how we are going to get through all of this."

Chapter One

WHY DO BAD THINGS HAPPEN TO GOOD PEOPLE?

Each year when Christmas rolls around, you know you're going to get at least one disappointing gift. You know who the giver will be, because every year he strikes out. Unspoken gift etiquette demands that even if a gift stinks you can't say, "Oh, how stupid!" Instead, you have to say, "Well ... *thanks!*" Anytime you say something negative about a gift, you get into trouble. "You should be grateful," say your friends. "After all, it's the thought that counts." I always want to respond, "Maybe they're not thinking hard enough."

A guy once handed me a department store gift certificate while blurting out, "Don't spend it all in one place!" I wanted to say, "It *is* a gift certificate, wing-nut. Duh! I can't really spread it around, can I?" Or maybe you asked for a designer gift only to get the knock-off version. You ask for a pair of Cole-Haan shoes and you end up getting Calhoun's. Or you wanted black Adidas but you got bright pink A-doo-doos.

I regularly speak at a Bible study in Oklahoma City, and the band members providing the music know I hate dumb gifts. One of my pet peeves is Christian T-shirts. I hate them because they are usually modeled after ripped-off corporate logos. Instead of *Budweiser,* these shirts change it to *Bewiser.* Instead of *Ford,* the logo says *Lord.* Instead of promoting *Coca Cola,* the artwork says *Jesus Christ, He's the Real Thing.*

So the band gave me a shirt with the *Rolling Stone* magazine logo on it that had been altered to say *Really Saved.* If that wasn't enough, they also gave me a pocket planner. But this was no ordinary pocket planner; it was a Christian pocket planner! (Perhaps it meant that each individual page had been led to the Lord?) I was afraid I might look inside and see that all the days of the week had been taken out and replaced with Sundays.

My point in all of this: The best part of Christmas is taking back all the gifts so you can get what you really want.

But you've got to keep the Christmas cards, which is another pain in the neck. Also, this is one area where men and women have completely different perspectives. A woman will take off work for half a day to go to Hallmark and read every card. It has to be the right color, the right height, and it has to say just the right thing. She has to dissect the words to find out what the meaning *really* is and then ponder to see if those are the words she *really* wants to say. She has to pick out just the right envelope and make sure the colors all match. After she practices her handwriting on a piece of scrap paper, she carefully writes the big loopy letters and caps off the ceremony with a spritz of perfume. Only then does she send this thing of beauty into the mail.

A guy, on the other hand, picks up a card while he's at the gas station. He'll cram the nozzle into the tank, squeeze the handle, and lock the pump into automatic. This gives him plenty of time to run inside and pick up a card (any card will do). He'll fill it out at the traffic light on his way over to his girlfriend's house. If he's lucky, the gas he spilled on his hands won't be quite dry, so he can use it to moisten the glue instead of licking the envelope. After all, you don't know how many hands have handled it.

By the way, isn't it amazing how Christmas is depicted on those Christmas cards? There are tranquil scenes with camels and wise men walking across the desert following a bright star. Or you see a picture of shepherds tending their sheep by moonlight, with everything drawn in varying shades of blues and blacks. So peaceful. Or the card displays a nativity scene with the baby Jesus in Mary's arms and Joseph standing behind her, dazed, wondering what just happened to him. In this one, lots of light cascades over the baby as everyone kneels around him. The traditional Christmas card centers on a pristine biblical scene.

At the other end of the spectrum, you find cards with pictures of Merry Old England and its Tudor homes, the heavy snow piling up on the eaves. There are candles whose light flickers through the windows, casting a golden glow on the snow beneath. These cards convey serenely happy, devotional auras.

As you can tell, I'm going to use the event of Christmas to launch us into our discussion on suffering. But suppose we step out of Christmas-greeting-card land and into Bible land for our beginning? As we read the real Christmas story, we find that the picture-card images do little to represent what actually took place that night. In fact, they're not even close.

Get the real story

When we read the story of Mary and Joseph, we find that it took place on an evening filled with fear and trepidation. Joseph had been ready to divorce Mary. She had become pregnant while they were still engaged ... and he knew for certain that it was not his child.

While Mary was nine months pregnant, the two had to complete the long journey to Bethlehem. When they arrived, there wasn't a vacant room anywhere, so they had to stay in the stables with all the animals. This was not a happy time.

> ❝ The pain of life began long ago, way past the edge of our experiential radar screen. ❞

This was not a peaceful time in the region, either. Fear filled the air. Because of his paranoia that another king would be born and take his position, Herod was searching to kill every male child in the land. In fact, the reason Mary and Joseph had gone to Bethlehem was on the orders of the government. Fear and intimidation permeated their lives.

How can we recapture what Christmas was really all about? How can we see the story of Christ's birth in a new light? How can we pull back the screen of all the happy pictures and Christmas carols so that we clearly see what went on that night?

I'd like to suggest an idea here, that there is a place in Scripture—other than the Gospels—that also tells the Christmas story. Consider this with me. It will help strip away everything that has gotten in the way of seeing the real Christmas. I'm talking about Revelation 12. There John has a vision that looks into history. He looks backward toward the coming of the Savior into this world. When we read this story, it will not at all reinforce the way we feel about the holidays.

You see, the pain of life began long ago, way past the edge of our experiential radar screen. Before humans were ever created and placed in the Garden of Eden, a battle took place in heaven, with God emerging victorious. The defeated beings were relocated to the earth, where their battle raged on.

When humans appeared on earth, the life they attempted to live became the prize that the defeated ones sought to gain. Down through the ages humankind has faced similar struggles in its search to live life to its fullest. Only Jesus has proven able to give life, defeat the enemy, and provide the means to lasting peace. His debut on earth is the real story of Christmas. And his life provides us with the context when we ask: "Why does life hurt so much?" Jesus dealt with the hurts of life in three decisive ways.

Jesus broke into history

To get the full effect of how far our expectations about Christmas are from its real meaning, try humming "Silent Night" to yourself while reading the following passage of Scripture:

> *A great sign appeared in heaven: a woman clothed with the sun, and the moon under her feet, and on her head a crown of twelve stars; and she was with child; and she cried out, being in labor and in pain to give birth. Then another sign appeared in heaven: and behold, a great red dragon having seven heads and ten horns, and on his heads were seven diadems. And his tail swept away a third of the stars of heaven and threw them to the earth. And the dragon stood before the woman who was about to give birth, so that when she gave birth he might devour her child. And she gave birth to a son, a male child, who is to rule all the nations with a rod of iron; and her child was caught up to God and to His throne. ...*
>
> *And there was war in heaven, Michael and his angels waging war with the dragon. The dragon and his angels waged war, and they were not strong enough, and there was no longer a place found for them in heaven. And the great dragon was thrown down, the serpent of old who is called the devil and Satan, who deceives the whole world; he was thrown down to the earth, and his angels were thrown down with him.*
>
> —Revelation 12:1–5, 7–9

What we read in the Gospels about the donkey ride to Bethlehem, and the manger birth, did physically happen in the world. Yet at the same time, in the spiritual realm, the account recorded in Revelation 12 was going on. That night was not a night of silence; it was a night of war. It was a night of cosmic conflict as battles raged in the heavenly realm. I believe that for us to really understand what Christmas is about, we must understand what John was saying in the Book of Revelation.

> **Evil was born in the heart of a being who had the power to choose.**

Evil was born in the heart of a being who had the power to choose. Lucifer was that being, the angel God had created and installed as an archangel and heaven's worship leader. This influential and powerful being succumbed to a personal ambition to replace God. He plotted to dethrone God and enlisted the aid of one-third of heaven's angels to help him. The battle that followed was so horrific the Scripture only tells us that Lucifer and a third of the angels were cast out of heaven and banished to the earth.

Scripture characterizes evil as a real being resisting God's creation. Evil is a fallen angel whose presence comes through in Scripture in different ways. Wherever it appears, it resists everything that is good in the world. Evil set itself to the task of de-creating everything God had created. Evil's resistance pervades our world. It can show up in many different ways, such as within a mindset ("I'm going to do my own thing"); within a political ideal (think of Hitler or Saddam Hussein); or within any ambition competing with God's initiative.

The apostle John reported seeing a red dragon waiting to devour the seed of the woman. In Scripture, this seed is Jesus—and everything that is born of God. Every life that has been born of God, every job, every ministry, and every relationship born of God will become a target of the enemy. Evil opposes everything associated with God's initiative.

> **Each of us has the power to actualize either God's initiative or the ambition of evil.**

Christ is the seed of God, and he came to establish his kingdom and reclaim the universe. That first Christmas night, the enemy failed to devour the seed. Instead, he now focuses on *the destruction of the produce of the seed* to keep it from reclaiming the world.

Many times the attacks we face are not personal, because they aren't waged directly against us. They are being waged at some part of the seed that is impacting our lives. I know a man who serves in a leadership role at his church. He is well qualified, having passed serious examination in order to serve in this capacity. Within thirty days of his taking leadership, his oldest child entered the hospital with an undiagnosed disease. It took his doctors two weeks, with multiple testings, to figure out what was wrong. Then it took several more weeks for the child to get well enough to go back to school. Only a month or two later this man's wife lost her job in a completely unexpected turn of events.

But this man's family wasn't the direct target of evil. The seed intersected their lives. More importantly, the seed intersected this man's life, and the enemy was resisting the growth of the seed. The enemy had set itself on destroying the seed, and this man and his family were caught in the crossfire. If this man were to resign his position of leadership, the attention of evil would shift somewhere else. But should he resign, he'd be choosing something other than the initiative of God for his life.

Each of us has the power to actualize either God's initiative or the ambition of evil. The impact of our choice determines the speed of growth experienced in the kingdom of God.

I heard a loud voice in heaven, saying, "Now the salvation, and the power, and the kingdom of our God and the authority of His Christ have come, for the accuser of our brethren has been thrown down, he who accuses them before our God day and night. And they overcame him because of the blood of the Lamb and because of the word of their testimony, and they did not love their life even when faced with death.

—Revelation 12:10–11

John saw a vision and repeated it from the perspective of the angels. God had safely delivered his Son into the world. Jesus came into the same world we are born into. It was a world filled with evil and suffering brought about by a being who willfully chose to de-create God's creation. Jesus had broken into our history. I call this the great Christmas invasion. It is God in the form of Jesus invading our world.

In that manger was God in human flesh breaking into human history. With him he brought salvation, power, and authority over the darkness. At the moment of Jesus' birth, everything real in heaven was made real on this earth. At that moment, everything alive and thriving in heaven came with Jesus and invaded this world.

> ❝ At the moment of Jesus' birth, everything real in heaven was made real on this earth. At that moment, everything alive and thriving in heaven came with Jesus and invaded this world. ❞

The Bible word for Jesus' breaking into this world is *incarnation*. He literally stepped out of heaven and into this world. Why is this so important? It's because at that moment, the very life of God invaded human history. For the first time, humanity and God co-existed in human flesh on the earth.

At that moment every event that could ever take place on this globe was exposed to the will of God. This was God stepping into the events of our planet. Therefore, from the moment of Jesus' birth until now, God has used history to display the growth of his kingdom. And he will continue to use history as his eternal canvas, because it is through history that we see God, feel him, experience him, and understand him. The message of Christmas is that Jesus is the only Son of God and that *his historical presence has changed everything.*

This was not simply a baby lying in a feeding trough. From this moment on, the impact of this one life would bring about the fulfillment of God's will. He broke into this world to establish his will and change the history of this world ... and the history of our lives.

He battled hostile forces

The entire focus of Revelation 12 is to help us see that Jesus came to earth for a key purpose: to do war. John was showing us that the evil force was not just a yard dog on a chain. The evil dragon held cosmic power.

> *And the serpent poured water like a river out of his mouth after the woman, so that he might cause her to be swept away with the flood. But the earth helped the woman, and the earth opened its mouth and drank up the river which the dragon poured out of his mouth. So the dragon was enraged with the woman, and went off to make war with the rest of her children, who keep the commandments of God and hold to the testimony of Jesus.*

—Revelation 12:15–17

The enemy focused on doing battle. He would make war against the woman and—guess who? The rest of her offspring, those who hold to Jesus.

Satan had already lost his position in heaven, and now that God had invaded the earth, he faced the very real potential of losing his earthly rule as well. When Jesus invaded the earth, the enemy (the red dragon), unleashed his attack on God's plan to redeem the universe and his people. Satan knew that Jesus had come to do battle with his hostile forces.

He began a holy community

Jesus broke into human history and began to build a holy generation. This would be his people, a community who would belong only to him and who would revolt against the ambition of evil.

> They overcame him because of the blood of the Lamb and because of the word of their testimony, and they did not love their life even when faced with death. "For this reason, rejoice, O heavens and you who dwell in them. Woe to the earth and the sea, because the devil has come down to you, having great wrath, knowing that he has only a short time."
> So the dragon was enraged with the woman, and went off to make war with the rest of her children, who keep the commandments of God and hold to the testimony of Jesus.
>
> —Revelation 12:11–12, 17

In verse 11 we read: "They overcame him." That is, the church overcame Satan. In verse 17 we read: "The dragon was enraged ... with the rest of her children." Her *children* are the community of faith.

Jesus would assemble his people and form the bride and the body of Christ on this earth. Jesus gives to his body the same weapons he used to battle the hostile forces. Jesus defeated the enemy's hold over the cosmos with his blood on the cross. When we

> ❝ It is not an individual war but a community war. Since his death, Jesus has been building a worldwide body. ❞

give our life to him, his victorious blood is given to us. Jesus shattered the grip of the enemy by his message, his Word. His message is now given to us.

As you can see, this is not an individual victory; it is a community victory. It is not an individual war but a community war. Since his death, Jesus has been building a worldwide body. It's a community that, together with him, will advance his kingdom until the will of God is being done on earth, just as it is being perfectly performed in heaven.

When we aren't connected to Christ's community, we become an easy target for the enemy. When we excuse ourselves from worshiping with believers and rationalize that we can meet with God just as well on the golf course or at the lake, we need to admit what we already know to be true:

We're wrong. The presence of God resides within the people of God. Church is where we're placed and planted. Through the church, we become a part of the community of God. It is in this community that we receive the power of God and instruction in the Word of God.

Seeing the birth of Jesus in this way makes us responsible. What are we going to do with this truth? Where are we going to plant our lives? Jesus knows that the enemy can devour individuals, but he has never been able to defeat the church. That's because the church is the community of Christ. When we meet together, we can take on the Word of Christ, the blood of Christ, and the abandonment he demonstrated by coming to this earth. Together, we become an unstoppable force.

There has to be a point that we take on the Word of Christ in our lives. The "brethren" of verse 11 overcame the enemy with the testimony of their word. The word of their testimony was backed up in the way they lived their lives. The word their lives demonstrated is that Jesus broke into human history, died on the cross, rose again, and is now the ruler and rightful king over heaven. We carry the same word in our bodies. Collectively, we have the opportunity to become powerful, living examples of the everyday

> **" Jesus knows that the enemy can devour individuals, but he has never been able to defeat the church. "**

presence of God in our world. The challenge is for us to rise up and become the people God wants us to be.

We have taken an insightful look into Revelation 12 and witnessed John looking back, seeing the fall of Satan, the birth of Christ, and the war on this earth. John's message to the church is that the battle continues. We cannot be neutral. We must choose sides. God has a place for us in

> ❝ Christmas is really about warfare, not finely wrapped gifts. It's about combat rather than big dinners and pretty lights. ❞

his kingdom, and that place is in his community, the church.

As we close this chapter, I hope you've seen how important Christmas is to our exploration of suffering and God's place in it. Christmas is really about warfare, not finely wrapped gifts. It's about combat rather than big dinners and pretty lights. So plant yourself in the battle. If you are not a Christian, open your life to Jesus, the Son of God, and let him break into your own life and rewrite your personal history. Join me in the battle, and together we will fight and live the way Jesus did.

Chapter Two

GOD, WHERE ARE YOU?

Recently I was asked to speak at a conference on postmodernism. I came in a day early so I decided to sit in the audience that night and listen to one of the speakers. This guy was a screamer. You know, a guy who yells and screams and ... calls it preaching. I grew up under that kind of preaching. The preachers would say things like, "You're going to die and go straight to hell."

Straight to hell—like some people get to stop off first. Did they really think God was going to point people out for that privilege? *"You* are going to die and go straight to hell while *you,* on the other hand, get to stop off and get a Slurpee." The speaker that night was saying some of those same crazy things and sprinkling in words like *brother, sister, yoo-hoo,* and *bless God* all through his message. He reminded me of the cartoon character Yosemite Sam getting all fired up about something. I was waiting for this guy to pull out his pistols and shoot the sky! I really thought to myself, *There's going to be a lynching.*

This guy's talk was filled with crazy Christian clichés. He said things like …

"God will turn your rough nights into righteous days."

"God doesn't grade on a curve; he grades on a cross!"

"When the devil reminds you of your past, remind him of his future."

"My God answers knee-mail."

"God's Instant Messenger is always on."

"Heaven's no trick and hell's no treat."

"You can't walk with God and hold hands with the devil at the same time."

"Give Satan an inch and he'll be the ruler."

"You can't beat the sin game—first it fascinates and then it assassinates."

"You can't play hopscotch with the devil; that's not going to work."

"Maybe you can fry an egg on the devil's backside, but I can guarantee it won't come out sunny side up!"

Everybody got so worked up over what this guy was saying that I thought they were going to start spiking hymnals. I sat back in disbelief. All that stuff was so full of cheese, if you poked it, it would bleed Velveeta.

The sad thing is, this guy's talk represents the bumper-sticker theology many of us have embraced. Much of what we know about God has been condensed into crazy little phrases like these. Anytime we face a problem, we pull out a little phrase and hope it helps. We've only picked up these theological bits and pieces because we've grown up where preachers screamed and shouted stuff like: "I've read the end of the book—and we win!"

Hearing such phrases doesn't necessarily draw us any closer to God. In fact, overexposure to them has produced a shallow Christianity and even caused some people to become bitter toward God. Some reading this book grew up in an atmosphere similar to mine and were expected to just "go along with it" and accept it like everyone else seemed to do.

> 66 If what they say is true, then where is God in the middle of my messed up life? There has been a disconnect of the truth from our experience. 99

Once you were old enough to choose for yourself, you bailed out.

For many, the lack of a practical theology has brought resentment. Who hasn't been to an "amen service" featuring a preacher who worked up enough sweat and spit to drench the first three pews—only to leave the service and return to a life filled with real pain, real suffering, and real sorrow? After that kind of church experience, who wouldn't think, "What's the deal? Why don't any of those phrases spill over into real life?" We look at the reality of our own lives in stark contrast to the crazy Yosemite Sam preachers. It makes us angry. It makes us wonder: If what they say is true, then where is God in the middle of my messed up life? There has been a disconnect of the truth from our experience.

Some people have grown bitter. Others who have heard these sayings have become passive. They aren't angry at the church or its leadership. They aren't even necessarily angry at God. They've just clicked off from God and the church.

Others have become fatalists because of what they've been taught. "Hey, we've read the end of the book, and we win, right?" So they just sit down and quit. They're waiting for Tim LaHaye to run out of books to write so we can all just go home to be with Jesus.

What did Jesus come to do? Did he come to yell at people? Did he come just to live, to die, and to live again so we can have more bumper stickers and little theological catch phrases? Is that all his presence on earth is about? I don't think so. To truly see how Jesus lived, and really hear what he said, is to hear the voice of God and see him in actions with which we can actually identify.

What did Jesus come to do?

Let's go back to Jesus and ask the central question, "What was Jesus' mission?" When we understand his mission, we can understand what's going on in our lives. We can also understand why we are still here and what we're supposed to do while we're on this earth. There is no way to take on the circumstances that life throws at us until we understand the role of Jesus, who he was and what he came to do.

While Jesus was on earth, he lived to fulfill the Father's

will. He didn't come to be a speaker, a poet, or a philosopher. He came to bring life! Jesus was on a mission, so he didn't come just because it was written in the script. Jesus came to accomplish something.

In Luke 4, Jesus had spent forty days in the desert, face to face with Satan. Forty days straight, facing your most lethal opponent: if that's not conflict, I don't know what is. The enemy threw his best shots at Jesus, tempting him with power, prestige, and legal ownership of all the kingdoms of the earth. Jesus defeated him by the Word of God.

A careless reading of this passage might give the impression that Jesus used some "catch phrases" in his battle with Satan. The truth is, his words flowed from his personal connection with God the Father. Jesus, the God-man—but living on earth according to his human nature—was so intimately bound to the Father that he knew the Father's words were true. Jesus had left heaven, "emptied" himself of the privileges of deity (see Phil. 2:7), and staked everything on those words' validity.

When Jesus left the wilderness encounter with Satan, he left complete. Satan was not able to take any part of Jesus' life, and Jesus walked away thoroughly victorious. This desert contest was the qualifying round for Jesus. He was beginning his public ministry, and he had successfully faced-down Satan. He was now ready to go to war on God's behalf.

Jesus came out of the desert and returned to his hometown, where he had already developed a reputation for being a teacher. The church leaders asked him to come and preach in his home synagogue. Jesus walked into the service,

> ❝ Jesus didn't come just to play the part of the hero in a cosmic drama. He had come on a rescue mission: to reclaim the ones who'd been caught in the enemy's crossfire. ❞

unrolled the Scripture scroll, and read a passage from Isaiah 61. (Luke is quoting this story in chapter 4 as his way of describing what really happened.)

The synagogue was the focal point of the community. The Pharisees had gained control of the synagogues and had imposed their own extremely legalistic form of religion there. Lots of religious activity surrounded the synagogue, but there was not much happening spiritually.

One of the key principles of potent leadership is that *the effectiveness of activity is directly proportionate to the clarity of mission.* When Jesus disclosed his mission for being on the earth, he was crystal clear:

> *"The Spirit of the Lord is upon Me, because He anointed Me to preach the gospel to the poor. He has sent Me to proclaim release to the captives, and recovery of sight to the blind, to set free those who are oppressed, to proclaim the favorable year of the Lord."*

And He closed the book, gave it back to the attendant and sat down; and the eyes of all in the synagogue were fixed on Him.

—Luke 4:18–20

This is a high drama situation. Jesus was reading from the Book of Isaiah, and he was speaking about himself. And everyone knew it. He finished speaking, rolled the scroll back up, and put it away. Every eye in the synagogue was on Jesus as he sat down. "And He began to say to them, 'Today this Scripture has been fulfilled in your hearing'" (Luke 4:21).

Jesus was extremely focused. He knew exactly what he had come to do, and he used this passage in Isaiah to declare his intentions. This passage teaches us three things about Jesus' purpose on earth.

He was as certain of the devil as he was of God

The types of people Jesus named as the focus of his ministry were the poor, the captives, the blind, and the oppressed. Jesus saw that these folks had been trounced with evil. He saw them as casualties in the war between light and dark. They were the captives of the enemy, blinded by the darkness, oppressed by evil. Satan had stolen their wealth. These weren't just "extras" written into a movie script starring God's Son. Jesus didn't come just to play the part of the hero in a cosmic drama. He had come on a rescue mission: to reclaim the ones who'd been caught in the enemy's crossfire.

Jesus was certain the devil was God's archenemy Let's make one point clear: The devil wasn't hired labor. God didn't hire the devil to perform random evil acts so he could send his Son to show off. The devil was not on contract with God; the devil was the enemy of God. Everything God loved, the devil hated. Everything God was doing, the devil tried to undo.

These were opposing forces, not friends. They weren't ever going to sit down and have a quiet dinner with each other. The devil was the archenemy of God.

Jesus was certain the devil authored all evil Let these next few thoughts sink deeply into your mind. Read them slowly. They may sound simplistic, but the truth they contain needs to saturate all of our thinking.

All evil originated from choices—really crummy choices. Freedom of will came from a good and loving God, which allowed the *possibility* of those bad choices. However, evil did not come from God. God didn't create evil to contrast his own goodness. He created freedom so his creatures could love him with whole hearts. And that's a good thing.

Satan and his angels chose to rebel against God's love and authority while they were in heaven. They were free moral agents who willfully decided to click off from God. Because Satan held some legal authority in the cosmos, he and his minions were able to wreak havoc in individuals' lives. Jesus knew that; there was no question in Jesus' mind what was going on. Jesus walked into the synagogue and read that

46

verse out of Isaiah to say unmistakably, "I am here to get my people back!"

Jesus was certain the devil attacks individuals Jesus knew that the enemy went after individuals. The proof was … the poor, the captives, the blind, and the oppressed on the earth. Their conditions cried out: We've been attacked! God was in the process of redeeming the whole universe, and Satan knew it—and was doing everything he could to stop it.

Some reading this book are struggling in marriages that are under attack. Others are embattled by finances in disarray, and personal dreams on the verge of destruction. These attacks aren't coming

> "God didn't create evil to contrast his own goodness. He created freedom so his creatures could love him with whole hearts."

from God; they're from the enemy. God is *not* setting you up to teach you some lesson. No, this attack is happening because God is at work in your life.

The enemy knows this, hates it, and will do anything he can to destroy that work. Just as Jesus entered a war for the earth, he knows we face many of the same battles.

The point is, Jesus never wondered where evil came from. He never looked for God's hidden purpose in evil, because it was never there. God didn't create the evil, so how could he have a purpose in it?

So can we quit blaming God for the bad things that have happened in our lives? So often we blame God for suffering, sickness, death, and disease when he is responsible for none of it. All of that comes from the enemy. Instead of ignoring it and acting as if it isn't there—or worse yet, passively accepting it as just an everyday part of life—we can remember that the darkness and evil isn't crashing down on us from heaven. It comes from the enemy, whose main purpose it is to de-create the work of God in this world and in your life.

> "" Evil has so infused our society that it has become quite acceptable ... as long as it's not more evil than I think is okay. ""

Jesus knows the world has been infested and polluted with evil. It's pervasive, not isolated in little pockets here and there. Even as it was in Jesus' day, evil has covered the earth, becoming so ingrained in us that we hardly notice it. We are born into it and, for the most part, we don't even recognize it.

We watch the news, little realizing that it's all about reporting evil. The producers categorize everything from the greatest evil to the smallest evil. Their guiding principle is: "If it bleeds it leads." So they open the broadcast with the most evil story of the day.

If we were to strip away the details of each nightly news

menu, we'd see that we're served up a never-ending dish of war, famine, death, AIDS, homelessness, depression, and economic recession. Then the news shifts from something evil to something silly: "And now a story about nachos." Then it moves to sports: wife beating, drug abuse, imprisonment, death, murder—all coming before the scores. Then it's the meteorologist's turn: hurricanes, earthquakes, storms, tsunamis. "And now, sunshine!" That's how the news works.

Political advertisements provide no relief. They point out evil. They use a variety of methods to communicate one simple message: "Don't trust this guy!" And then the small print at the bottom of the TV screen says, "Paid for by the other guy." Evil has so infused our society that it has become quite acceptable ... as long as it's not more evil than I think is okay. We have begun to think this way by categorizing things that are more evil and less evil. Then we step back and consider: *Just how much evil am I willing to tolerate?*

None of us are unaffected by evil. None of those who heard Jesus speak at the synagogue that day were unaffected by evil either. Like us, they lived in a world dominated by evil. Jesus understood all of this and was not shocked, he was not ashamed, and he was not fearful. He knew it, and he came to do something about it.

Jesus came to defeat evil

Look again at Luke 4:18–19, and pay attention to the words describing what Jesus came to do:

- to **proclaim** release;

- **recovery** of sight;
- to **set free**;
- to **proclaim** the favorable.

These words describe Jesus coming to defeat evil! Jesus did not come to teach people a hidden lesson. He didn't say, "God has a special seminar in this evil experience that he wants you to attend." In Jesus' mind, the world had been taken over by rebel forces that he must defeat. That's why Jesus stood up in the synagogue and said, "I've come to preach salvation from sin, to make blind eyes see, and to get people out of jail." Yes, Jesus came to defeat evil. How did he do it?

- Through his messiahship:

"... because [God] anointed me" (v. 18).

Jesus did what only the Messiah could do because he *was* the Messiah. There was no ego involved in his declaration. He was making the truth known that the Messiah had come to enforce his Father's attack on darkness. The only one who could recover sight for the blind, set the captives free, and liberate the oppressed was the Messiah.

The phrase "anointed one" implies that he was the *one* who could break

> **He didn't win because he was a great teacher, a beloved poet, or a mighty prophet; he defeated the devil because he was the Messiah.**

off all of the burdens. He is still the one who alone can carry away the baggage of our lives. Jesus was saying, "I have the power to come to this earth and take away every burden that the enemy has placed on people and to carry every piece of baggage that people are lugging around in their lives."

Jesus was able to defeat the devil because of who he (Jesus) was. He didn't win because he was a great teacher, a beloved poet, or a mighty prophet; he defeated the devil because he was the Messiah.

- Through his message
  "... to preach the gospel" (v. 18).

Jesus traveled throughout the region preaching. His message was: "The kingdom of God has come." He preached that there was a way out of the darkness and used analogies to make the purpose of the kingdom understandable—

- The kingdom is like a mustard seed that a man planted in his field. It is the smallest of all seeds, but it produces a very large plant.
- The kingdom is like yeast. A small amount is all you need to make the whole loaf of bread rise.
- The kingdom is like a treasure a man found in a field. He sold everything he had so he could buy that field and claim the treasure as his own.
- The kingdom is like a great fishing net catching all kinds of things. The separation takes place after the net is hauled ashore.

In these analogies, Jesus was saying ...

- "Don't let the size of what I'm doing mislead you. The seeds I'm planting may seem small, but they will produce goodness throughout the world."
- "The world is filled with evil, but it only takes a small amount of my work in you to affect the entire world."
- "Getting involved in the Father's initiative for the earth is more valuable than anything we can ever hope of producing for ourselves. If you have to sell everything to get involved, do it."
- "My task is to establish the kingdom of God throughout the earth, in the face of evil. Evil will not be completely removed until the day of the Lord finally arrives."

The message of Christ was complete and unified. Everything he taught demonstrated that his purpose was to complete the initiative of heaven.

- Through his ministry and miracles:
  "... they were amazed at His teaching, for His message was with authority" (Luke 4:32).

Jesus demonstrated with his works what he had spoken in his words. Instead of speaking in clichés, he spoke with weighty authority. When the people heard his words, they said to each other, "Listen to the authority this man speaks with." Later that same day, Jesus demonstrated his authority by casting the demon out of a man attending the synagogue.

In the synagogue there was a man possessed by the spirit of an unclean demon, and he cried out with a loud voice, "Let us alone! What business do we have with each other, Jesus of Nazareth? Have You come to destroy us? I know who You are—the Holy One of God!" But Jesus rebuked him, saying, "Be quiet and come out of him!" And when the demon had thrown him down in the midst of the people, he came out of him without doing him any harm.

And amazement came upon them all, and they began talking with one another saying, "What is this message? For with authority and power He commands the unclean spirits and they come out."

—Luke 4:33–36

Immediately after this, Jesus led his disciples to Peter's house, where he further demonstrated that his mission was to defeat evil.

Then he got up and left the synagogue, and entered Simon's home. Now Simon's mother-in-law was suffering from a high fever, and they asked him to help her. And standing over her, He rebuked the fever, and it left her; and she immediately got up and waited on them.

—Luke 4:38–39

Jesus didn't do these miracles as part of a show. No, he was driving out evil, reaching out to those who were hurting.

While the sun was setting, all those who had any
who were sick with various diseases brought them to
Him; and laying His hands on each one of them, He was
healing them. Demons also were coming out of many,
shouting, "You are the Son of God!" But rebuking them,
He would not allow them to speak, because they knew
Him to be the Christ.

—Luke 4:40–41

Jesus went about rebuking demons and setting people free. Everywhere he went, he demonstrated the power of the kingdom. He was not working in concert with the enemy; he was working against it. He was not cooperating with hell; he was working to defeat it. The rebel forces had oppressed and possessed the world, and Jesus had come to get the world back.

He canceled the dominion of evil

Jesus took away the control evil held over the universe. Satan and his cohorts were like the Cosmic Mafia; they had set up their racket around the earth, and Jesus came to take their territory away.

Look at the final line of Jesus' address in the synagogue, "To proclaim the favorable year of the Lord" (Luke 4:19). In the Old Testament, the day of Jubilee was the day when all debts were canceled and all the differences between enemies were reconciled. When Jesus read this, he was speaking of his ministry and his kingdom. Jesus was saying, "Today, in your hearing, the kingdom of God has come to earth in me to banish all the enemies and to cancel all the debts." Just imagine how radical this statement would sound to the people.

Jesus wasn't trying to get people to pray a little prayer or to have a nice feeling of security. He was letting them know that he was there to fight for their total and complete freedom from the bondage of darkness. Jesus was teaching that his kingdom would be established over and above the kingdom of darkness. The kingdom of Jesus would be about total freedom.

Jesus canceled the dominion of evil in eternity We tend to think that Christianity is all about us. We believe God went through everything he did just so we could pray "the sinner's prayer." While it is true that in the cross we can have eternal life in Christ, there's a bigger picture. What makes Jesus' ministry so powerful for us is that he places Satan center stage as the cause of all evil. When Jesus saw evil, he didn't see it operating legally underneath the providence of God. The picture Jesus paints for us is that evil existed in complete opposition to God's initiative.

Much of our day's popular theology teaches us that God won't allow us to experience more evil than we can withstand. At first reading, this sounds good. After all, God is all-powerful, and he is in full control of his creation. So we easily believe that the hand of God completely encircles evil, ready to stop it short before it brings us more than we could bear. Believing this gives us a warm, cozy feeling. We know God will allow evil to approach only so close to our lives before a hedge of protection stops it.

The problem is, Jesus taught something completely different. Today's theology removes Satan from the equation by limiting his ability to wreak havoc only to the extent controllable and allowable by God. Is it any wonder that we have become a generation of fatalists?

- "What difference does it make what I believe, if it's all going to work out in the end?"
- "What difference does it make what I believe, if God's got it all scripted out?"
- "What difference will my life make? God is able to make anything work out for the good, regardless of whoever needs it."

Jesus' ministry spotlights Satan as the inventor of evil, the designer of de-creation, and the cause of chaos in our world. Jesus came to do more than recite memorized lines to God's cosmic play. He came to completely enforce heaven's initiative against the autonomous forces of darkness.

Jesus canceled the dominion of evil every day The "favorable year of the Lord" is not just about eternity. Every single day the life of Christ impacts our lives. Becoming a follower of Christ is not just about missing hell and making heaven; rather, it's about what happens to us on a daily basis. Following Christ is saying, "God, you own the title deed of life."

The title for a piece of property has to be cleared of any outstanding debts before a new owner can receive it. When we become a Christ follower, all outstanding connections to evil are removed. The title for our life is unattached to anything other than the cross of Christ. Our destiny has been changed from the inside out. Once we were children of the kingdom of darkness; now we are children of the kingdom of light. And we live according to the reality of our new status. Without the life of Christ living in us, we are destined to fall back into darkness and repeat our old patterns and problems. We need the "favor" of life-in-Christ every day on this earth, not just in eternity.

Jesus canceled the dominion of evil for everyone Jesus offers life to everyone. He came to redeem the entire world and everyone in it. The Bible makes certain we understand this truth.

Matthew wrote his gospel to the Jews, but Luke wrote to the Gentiles and anyone else who wasn't a Jew by birth. Luke showed that Jesus didn't come to offer his ministry only to one group of people, but to offer his gift of life to everyone. Luke shows us

> ❝The question is, 'Where is God?' The answer is, he is exactly where he has always been, actively opposing the source and cause of suffering, pain, and evil.❞

that the good, the bad, the right, and the wrong could come to the Lord. A person's color, tribe, or nation didn't matter. Anyone could experience the life of Christ. Anyone could have her enemies defeated, her debts cancelled, and her soul made whole.

Jesus came to earth to defeat the virus of evil. His motive for preaching, healing, and performing miracles was to bring the ambition of resistance to an end. Jesus was establishing his kingdom, putting into motion something that continues to spread throughout the globe to this day. There is no question evil still plunders the earth; but its grip over humanity has been stripped away. The enemy causes suffering, and all his underlings still wreak havoc on the population. But in the midst of our struggles, Jesus enters and confronts the resistance on our behalf.

He is the Lord of the earth, but countless battles rage in the lives of his people. Any of us who are trapped, caught in destructive behavior, depressed, or sick, tired, and struggling—or questioning his goodness—can connect with the presence of Christ and experience the victory. He can and will drive out evil in our lives and take captive anything that has taken hold of us.

He is the God who never leaves us alone. He is the compassionate God who continually seeks us out, who cares enough not to just let the world go to hell. He sent his only Son to break into human history and do ultimate battle with evil. He has won the right for every one of us to connect with him personally and to break ranks with Satan's resistance so we can join the kingdom of light.

The question is, "Where is God?" The answer is, he is exactly where he has always been, actively opposing the source and cause of suffering, pain, and evil.

The things Jesus declared at the beginning of his ministry, he lived out and demonstrated through his words and actions. They were much more than theories and ideas; they shaped his entire ministry.

Chapter Three

Is God Trying to Teach Me Something Through This?

My mom is an Internet junkie, and she loves to order things online. As a result, packages keep showing up at the house, and I have no idea what part of cyberspace they came from. (My mom and the UPS man are getting along quite nicely. Thanks for asking.)

One of the recent arrivals was an emergency weather device. Since we have so many tornadoes in Oklahoma, it should come in handy. It has a fog light on the back, an ear wax cleaner on the right side, a siren protruding from the top, an AM/FM radio (with both big and little holes for private musical enjoyment), a flashlight and blinking smaller lights that alternate yellow and red, as well as a three-inch television screen.

The TV and the flashlight are on the same side. How is that going to help me? I guess if I need to go outside and look for a burglar, I can search the bushes with the flashlight while hollering, "Come on out. *Friends* is on, and we can watch it together!"

Once you order something from the Internet, your name gets placed on myriad solicitation lists for all kinds of crazy products. Those companies even send us magazines because they heard we like to buy pointless junk. I take these magazines on trips so I can look through them on the airplane. I'm amazed. Some companies make product combinations that just don't make sense to me: a sweater vest that doubles as a can opener, a thermos that's also a snorkel, and a battery-powered cassette player that's also a dog.

Sadly, our fascination with gadgets has infected the way we form our theology. Too much of our theology has been created from bits and pieces of information that are, at best, nondescript. We've heard people from all walks of life talk about God based on their ... experiences. The result, for many of us, is that our whole belief system—regarding God, suffering, evil, and the world—rides upon little snippets of ideas we've picked up from here and there. One person says, "I heard that God causes all kinds of sickness so he can bring healing and make himself look good." One would-be sage I heard just today said, "God writes many a lesson on the blackboard of affliction."

66 Lots of people are angry with God because they've chosen to believe things about him that just aren't true. 99

We have taken some pretty crazy word-gadgets and accepted them as truth, because we don't know the difference. But many of these false beliefs have become the source of anger against God. Lots of people are angry with God because they've chosen to believe things about him that just aren't true. Some are angry with God because they've believed untruths regarding the way he relates to the world and the events of their lives. As a result, the smorgasbord of ideas about God and theology has blocked the abundance available through the life Jesus gave us.

Perhaps there's little urgency or purpose to our lives because we ingest so many theological tidbits from the buffet line of random teachings available 24/7 from such wholesome sources as Christian television programming. This rather suspect snack shop of theological cuisine offers half-baked goodies served up by any number of Bible butchers. They wield their Benihana styles of Scripture interpretation like Japanese chefs. They slice and dice the truth until it's barely recognizable.

In other words, we can always find someone who will teach us anything we want to believe. If it's not a recipe we favor, wait thirty minutes. The next teacher is sure to dish out something we'll consider a marvelous soup du jour.

Or do we need to reformat our assumptions about life and God? Could we revisit how we arrived at our understandings of suffering, pain, and evil—and recover the New Testament understanding of these things?

We might begin by remembering that Jesus saw the whole globe engaged in a conflict between light and dark. This drove Jesus to do what he did, to enter this world and turn it upside down in only three years of public ministry. This truth was the secret to his effectiveness, and it is our source of hope in the midst of suffering. We need to discover it for ourselves and load it into our lives.

> *They came to the other side of the sea, into the country of the Gerasenes. And when He had come out of the boat, immediately a man from the tombs with an unclean spirit met Him, and he had his dwelling among the tombs. And no one was able to bind him anymore, even with a chain; because he had often been bound with shackles and chains, and the chains had been torn apart by him, and the shackles broken in pieces, and no one was strong enough to subdue him.*
>
> *And constantly, night and day, he was screaming among the tombs and in the mountains and gashing himself with stones. Seeing Jesus from a distance, he ran up and bowed down before Him; and shouting with a loud voice, he said, "What business do we have with each other, Jesus, Son of the Most High God? I implore You by God, do not torment me!"*
>
> —Mark 5:1–7

Jesus clearly understood the condition of the world and humankind. He didn't insulate himself with cynicism or silliness when facing reality. Through his unsheltered eyes he saw the chaos of the world. He used his bare hands to touch the sewage swirling amidst human existence, and he never lost hope. He was able to live in the midst of the suffering and chaos of the darkness because of what he believed about the world and people. Even though there are no clean, clever answers to pain and suffering, there is a way to face evil and to handle it. It's the way Jesus did it.

Jesus had the heart of a fighter. Before his public ministry he was a well-respected member of the Nazareth community. But once he started preaching, he faced untold opposition from friends, family,

> **"Even though there are no clean, clever answers to pain and suffering, there is a way to face evil and to handle it.""**

and total strangers. Jesus could have chosen a different path, but it would have led him to a much different history. No, he had the heart of a fighter. His gloves-off, no-holds-barred way of dealing with evil comes through in three specific ways.

Jesus expected hell on earth

Jesus and his disciples traveled across the lake only to come ashore and face a maniac. Notice that Jesus wasn't shocked by this man's condition. He knew evil operated in this world. He knew a rebel force was de-creating what he'd created. When Jesus came, he expected to find hell on earth … and he had found it. So, the man standing before him was being torn apart by evil.

None of us should be shocked by a world saturated with evil. We need to quit being embarrassed by the fact that evil runs rampant around us. The rebel force has the power of choice, and it is always after us, intent on undoing the will of God for our lives. Jesus understood this.

It's easy to spot the large and obvious signs of evil—all the war, sickness, famine, abuse, poverty, and malice. But our world swarms with *subtle* evidences. This is why we outlaw toy guns but sell real ones at Wal-Mart. We tell kids not to play in the street, and then we sell ice cream from a moving truck. In large and small ways we are all affected by this rebel force penetrating our world. When Jesus encountered sickness, disease, blindness, and deaf mutes, not once did he try to find the mysterious reason God allowed these things to happen. In his warrior heart, he knew what he faced. Jesus expected hell on earth, and he came to overthrow it.

> Jesus expected hell on earth, and he came to overthrow it.

Jesus looked at this demon-possessed man and saw a simple truth: The will of God is not being done in this man's life. If Jesus invaded earth to face down evil, then this was a prime opportunity.

Jesus excused the hurting

Have you noticed that Jesus constantly waded into these types of situations? Regardless of where he traveled, he cast out demons, healed the blind and lame and mute, touched and healed scores of lepers. When Jesus entered a scene, the effects of evil rose up to meet him. From verses 5 and following, Jesus began to deal with the demonic spirit residing inside the man.

> He was asking him, "What is your name?" And he
> said to Him, "My name is Legion; for we are many." And
> he began to implore Him earnestly not to send them out
> of the country.
>
> —Mark 5:9–10

These evil spirits were on assignment and didn't want to leave. Yet they recognized Jesus for who he was and knew they must obey his orders. Notice that Jesus spoke to the spirits, distinguishing between the man himself and the spirits inside him. Jesus saw people in need of freedom as casualties of war. The planet was a war zone. Darkness had fallen upon the cosmos, ripping it apart, and some of the innocent fell wounded in the crossfire.

Some casualties of this war are reading this book. Some have been hurt by others, with physical or sexual abuse, rape, mental or emotional cruelty, divorce, adultery, or sickness. These things make us ask, "Why, God?"

But these things don't come from God.

A friend of mine called and asked me to speak to his home Bible study group. The members of this group had begun to share some of the hurts they had grown up with. A family member had abused one woman in the group, but her whole family had ignored the issue and treated her as if it had never happened. She had openly shared her pain and her anger toward God. She asked the group to pray for her so she could understand. She was plagued by questions like:

"Why did God allow this to happen to me?"
"How could God let him get away with what he did?"
"What is God trying to teach me through this?"

I was willing to address the group and did so with great care. I carefully considered all their feelings and lovingly conveyed some of the truths I am sharing in this book. Sometime during our evening together, I made this point: "God is not doing these things to us." Later, I was told it was this one sentence that helped turn that woman's life around. She stopped blaming God and began laying blame where it belonged: at the source of evil in this world. There is an evil force driving those who hand out our pain. We have been caught in the crossfire of the war between light and dark.

> 66 Not once will we ever find Jesus looking down at someone who has come to him for help and saying, 'Well, now you've gone and done it!' 99

Not once in this story does Jesus say to the demon-hounded man, "Now before I set you free from the evil spirits, have you learned your lesson? Have you learned anything from being made to live here in the cemetery? Have those chains taught you anything?" Nor did he say: "Before

I set you free we need to say a prayer. First, I'll say a line and then you'll repeat what I just said. Okay?" Jesus never required anything from the hurting except that they be present with their pain.

Not once will we ever find Jesus looking down at someone who has come to him for help and saying, "Well, now you've gone and done it! What am I going to do with you? Alright, come over here so I can make it all better." Yet some of us have been to churches where we've been shamed because of our lifestyle or habits. People who think they have the answers have gotten in our face and "confronted us in the Lord." But the Lord isn't like that. He doesn't assign blame to this guy, and he won't assign blame to us. Instead, Jesus uses his power and his faith to deliver the hurting.

Jesus excused the hurting and didn't assign blame, but this doesn't give us the freedom to excuse ourselves. We aren't free to say, "Hey, my life's screwed up, and it's okay with God. So I'm alright with things just the way they are." Excusing the hurting is a right granted only to Jesus. He has invaded this world to excuse us, not blame us. He has come to face down the enemy in our lives. This is the heart of a fighter, one who fights on our behalf to set us free.

We need to share Jesus' view of the way things are in this world. This will help us to quit judging people and stop being so quick to point out their problems. All around us are people whose lives have been destroyed by the work of the rebel force. One reason church is so important is because going to church is an act of war. We don't just attend to sing songs and fill in preaching outline blanks. Every person we bring is pulled out of darkness and put in a place where he can touch the presence of God for himself. When believers gather, they are in a place where the Holy One can come and deliver them.

We shouldn't invite our friends because the church needs a lot of people. We should bring them because we are challenging the forces of darkness, and they need to see the light. We are contending for the souls of every man, woman, and child, whether married, single, old, or young. With the church we have a better chance of defeating the darkness.

As reclaimed people who are reclaiming their world, we act with compassion for the hurting and tolerance for ourselves when we falter or fail. It helps us find the balance Jesus demonstrated when facing evil. It gives us his clarity to put blame in its proper place.

Jesus expelled the hold of evil

Now back to our story of the man with demons ...

He began to implore Him earnestly not to send them out of the country.

Now there was a large herd of swine feeding nearby on the mountain. The demons implored Him, saying, "Send us into the swine so that we may enter them." Jesus gave them permission. And coming out, the unclean spirits entered the swine; and the herd rushed down the steep bank into the sea, about two thousand of them; and they were drowned in the sea.

—Mark 5:10–13

70

These evil spirits were territorial, having been assigned to rule that particular region. Jesus simply approached the man and spoke with the demonic spirits. The spirits knew who Jesus was. In fact, they asked him what business they had with each other. Jesus gave them a simple response: hell. The demons were anxious. Confronted by Jesus, they had no idea what God was up to. All they knew was that they had no chance in a face-off with Jesus. So they came up with the bright idea that maybe Jesus would let them live in the pigs. Jesus granted their request.

But the pigs went crazy. What a demonstration of the sheer, raw power of evil! The spirits enter the pigs, and immediately the pigs commit group suicide. They rush down an embankment and drown. Jesus had expelled the hold of evil. To Christ, hell was not just a place but a real force on earth that had to be confronted and overcome.

Do we see hell the way Jesus did? Consider the way we use the word. Not long ago I was in Georgia eating at one of those 24-hour places like Denny's that's "always open" (why don't they add to the slogan, "and always dirty"?). I was eating with some friends, and they introduced me to one of the waitresses by telling her, "Dave is in town for a few days to speak at our church."

She responded with a smile, "Really, what church?"

I told her and asked her a simple follow-up question, "Do you go to church?"

"Sure I do."

"So where do you attend?"

She grabbed her head as if she were thinking very hard while mumbling, "What the hell is the name of that church?"

I fought to keep a straight face, but I appreciated her honesty. Apparently, we think hell has all the answers. When we're driving in traffic, we ask ...

"What the hell is that guy doing up there?"

"Who the hell does this guy think he is?"

"Where the hell is this guy going—look at him!"

"Oh, great! How the hell am I ever going to change lanes now?"

"Why the hell does it take me so long to get out of the church parking lot?"

We use "hell" as an adjective, too: "They are ugly as hell" or "That guy is as dumb as hell." But is it true there will only be ugly, dumb people in hell?

> 66 People like to say they're going out to raise some hell. Is that really the best use of our time—raising hell? 99

Or we say things like "bat out of hell." But are there other mammals in hell? Certainly dogs aren't in hell, because we know that all dogs go to heaven. (It must be true; there's a movie about it.) So maybe only bats and cats populate the netherworld? People like to say they're going out to raise some hell. Is that really the best use of our time—raising hell?

At a retreat, a guy told me, "Man, that was a hell of a sermon!" I wasn't quite sure how to take that. Then he said, "You scared the hell out of me!" What does that mean? Was that his salvation experience? Was that his moment of conversion? It's a good thing to have the hell scared out of you, isn't it? Finally, two hellish phrases seem forever linked with my dating life: "It's as cold as hell," and "That'll happen when hell freezes over."

> **"Two hellish phrases seem forever linked with my dating life: 'It's as cold as hell,' and 'That'll happen when hell freezes over.'"**

Anyway ... Jesus faced a legion of hellions in this man. In Bible terms, a legion is about six thousand. Jesus is taking on these thousands of evil spirits all at once. That's why the swine flipped out and said, "Let's get outta here!"

Jesus came against evil spirits and fought on behalf of this man, expelling evil. To Jesus, a reclaimed life was a free life! When someone came into the kingdom that person was restored to total mental, physical, and spiritual freedom. Look at how the story ends: "They came to Jesus and observed the man who had been demon-possessed sitting down, clothed and in his right mind, the very man who had had the 'legion'; and they became frightened" (Mark 5:15).

Here is the man who had once terrorized their town. Now he's sitting there in his right mind, fully clothed, and carrying on a normal conversation with Jesus. Jesus had given this man back his identity, his purpose, and his place in society. Jesus had restored this man's life! Restoring life is what Christ has always done.

Wherever there was hatred, apathy, racism, injury, and pain; wherever there was physical or psychological suffering, Jesus opposed it and overthrew it. This is how we must deal with evil. Instead of giving up and simply asking, "What is God trying to teach me through this?" or merely looking for the good he will bring out of it, we must begin to stand up and say, "Wherever there is evil, that is where the will of God is *not* being done."

> 66 **Wherever there was hatred, apathy, racism, injury, and pain; wherever there was physical or psychological suffering, Jesus opposed it and overthrew it.** 99

Jesus came to reclaim his territory and his people. He expected to find evil, and he did. He wasn't shocked by it, nor did he allow it to keep him from carrying out his mission. He came and excused the hurting and delivered the ones in need. We are his people, and his warrior heart rests in us. It is time that we ask him to awaken the warrior heart in us all. It is time for us to face evil when it is identified. When Christ shows up, hell has to leave. When Jesus walks in, hell loses its hold. It is God's will for us to live with the heart of a fighter.

And we will win the fight. For Jesus, our pain could never overtake the breadth and depth of God's goodness. Yet I know some of you are still asking, "How can God really be good when there is so much suffering and hurt in the world?" Jesus never offered simple platitudes. Instead, he pointed to God's faithfulness and goodness as the ultimate *context* for our struggles. Within that context we must answer for ourselves the question that forms the title of our next chapter.

Chapter Four

How good is God, really?

When my high school announced that it was starting a wrestling team, I really got excited and signed up. The first day of practice, I showed up wearing a cape and gold boots. (You see, I grew up watching pro wrestling at home on TV. Looking back, I wish I'd realized that the "outfits" in the high school version were a little less ... colorful.)

Now with my speaking, I'm on the road every week. Sometimes when I'm looking for a little drama on the television, I switch to wrestling. I don't really keep up with the characters' stories; I just like the over-the-top performances—especially since there's always a "back story" telling why certain wrestlers are angry with each other. I'm not much into the violence of wrestling. I just like to try and figure out what everyone is so upset about.

I don't understand boxing, though. I never can figure out what the two fighters are so angry about that they want to beat each other to a pulp. They enter the ring mad and never tell you why. Did the bald-headed guy in the blue-striped

> **Without the back story, the Gospels read like an impromptu convalescent tour that Jesus took so he could heal the sick, raise the dead, open blind eyes, and provide a few free lunches to the masses.**

trunks crash into the other guy's car in the parking lot? Did one guy steal the other guy's girl—or insult his mother? It seems to me that the two boxers climb into the ring already greased up and begin to beat on each other for no apparent reason. I like wrestling because the wrestlers at least tell you why they're mad at each other. They give you the back story.

When it comes to Christianity, few people feel a great deal of urgency. Could it be because they don't know the story behind the story?

Know the back story

Christianity can seem like a long list of things to do: sing, read the Bible, witness, pray, feel good, etc. If we're not careful, we can perpetuate the belief that it's all about becoming a better and nicer person.

Without the back story, the Gospels read like an impromptu convalescent tour that Jesus took so he could heal the sick, raise the dead, open blind eyes, and provide a few free lunches to the masses. Without the back story, we know Jesus told little parables with object lessons about seeds, coins, and pearls. The stories angered certain religious people, so they devised a plot and had him killed.

Without the back story, the Bible is a collection of interesting stories that hold our attention until we get old enough or brave enough to begin thinking for ourselves. At that point, the Bible begins to lose credibility, and any hope of having a practical application for our lives seems to vanish. That's why the back story is so important.

There is one thing that places everything Jesus did into context. It is the one thing that only he could bring with him that could cause the everlasting change the world needed. When Jesus entered the kingdom of darkness, he brought with him a kingdom not of this world to defeat it.

> **His kingdom will move us beyond the simple reordering of our behaviors.**

His kingdom would open the world to the goodness of God and provide people with the way to understand and respond to human suffering.

When Jesus looked at our dark world he saw a theater of war. The authors of the New Testament had the same vision and shared Jesus' mindset with us through their writings. When we finally begin to see Jesus' kingdom as they did, the difficult things about the Christian life take on an understandable context. His kingdom will move us beyond the simple reordering of our behaviors. It will give us context and

❝ When bad things happen, is God good? ❞

understanding into what God is doing on the earth. It will give us perspective in the midst of our personal suffering. Then, instead of reacting toward the specifics of the situation or the other people involved (or God), we can understand the true relevance behind the painful event. We can then face the trouble minus the anger.

The question behind "Why is this happening to me?" is this: "When bad things happen, is God good?" In other words, whenever we ask the "Why" question, we are really asking a lot of other questions, such as:

"Is God out to get me?"
"Is God out to teach me a lesson?"
"Is God allowing this for a reason?"

One pastor I know begins each worship time by leading the people in a responsive affirmation about God's goodness. He begins, "God is good," and the people respond, "All the time!" Then he turns it around and says, "All the time," and the people join in by saying, "God is good!"

This sounds good, and most of the people taking part in this verbal ring-around-the-rosy are all too happy to repeat the ritual week after week. But some of these same people, in the days after a worship service, will deny the goodness of God. They'll attribute to God the bad things that tumble into their lives.

Whether or not they recognize it, people like this pass judgment on God when they claim that he had some part in the bad things they experience. They try and figure out what lesson God is trying to teach them through the suffering. They question why God would be allowing them to face such a thing. They may even secretly, and sometimes openly, question how God could *cause* such a bad thing to happen.

So, on Sunday they proudly proclaim that "God is good all the time," but on Monday morning they believe that God's DNA has somehow been contaminated with strands of evil. In that hour on Sunday mornings, God is consistently all good—it's the rest of the week that he needs to work on. Their words on Sunday morning deny their hearts' attitudes the rest of the week. If they really spoke what they meant, when the pastor said, "God is good," the people would respond, "Except when my neighbor's kid gets cancer, my boss fires me, or airplanes fly into buildings."

> **In that hour on Sunday mornings, God is consistently all good—it's the rest of the week that he needs to work on.**

This thinking permeates the church in America. It has survived so long, and become such a part of our normal thinking, that we're spiritual schizophrenics when it comes to the goodness of God. Many of our frustrations about living our faith flow from our inaccurate concept of God. As we examine the kingdom of Jesus, one thing becomes abundantly clear: God really is good all the time. If this is unclear to you in any way, let me see if I can make it super simple. God is *all* good and the devil is *all* bad … *all* the time.

After I've delivered talks on this topic, people have flipped out and flooded my e-mail account with messages. Their e-mails agree that God is *all* good and that the devil is *all* bad, but they take issue with me when I say that God does not cause evil or use it to teach us lessons.

They ask me where I got this teaching. I tell them I started reading the Bible! I went back to the back story.

> **Jesus was God in the flesh. Therefore, he was as God is … *all* good.**

When you carefully read what the Bible says about Jesus, you see that he never used evil to make his point; instead, he always fought evil with everything he did and said. Jesus never caused anyone to be sick or crippled; he healed those people as a demonstration that his kingdom had come. Jesus never told half-truths that could mislead the masses; he spoke clearly so that "those who had ears" could hear the truth—that he had come to establish his kingdom and liberate the world.

Jesus was God in the flesh. Therefore, he was as God is … *all* good. He came to wage God's war against the darkness and the forces of evil. Could he then use evil to defeat evil and still remain all good?

It's all about the kingdom

It was through Christ that God destroyed the legal claim evil had on the earth. To believe God uses evil to teach us lessons is to believe that

> **66 To believe God uses evil to teach us lessons is to believe that God places a value on evil! ... Nothing could be further from the truth. God has no part of evil. 99**

God places a value on evil! It's to believe that God willfully includes evil in his divine plan for our spiritual growth. Nothing could be further from the truth. God has no part of evil.

Jesus came to establish his kingdom, and his kingdom was about setting people free. (When the Bible uses the word *kingdom*, it is always speaking of God's desire, intent, or goal.) To accomplish this he waged war against the darkness. In order to understand Jesus' view of the kingdom, we need to understand what he meant by the word *kingdom*. In Jesus' mind, the kingdom and God's will are one and the same. God's will was the kingdom, and Jesus came to establish God's will (or the kingdom) on earth.

Over the past several centuries, there have emerged many different understandings of God's relation to evil. But

> 66 Any city or house divided against itself will not stand. 99

can't we agree that Jesus has the authoritative view on this subject? That's why I will use his words as recorded in Scripture while being careful not to read beyond the text. One place we can see Jesus' "warfare worldview" comes in Matthew 12:

Then a demon-possessed man who was blind and mute was brought to Jesus, and He healed him, so that the mute man spoke and saw. All the crowds were amazed, and were saying, "This man cannot be the Son of David, can he?"

But when the Pharisees heard this, they said, "This man casts out demons only by Beelzebul the ruler of the demons."

And knowing their thoughts Jesus said to them, "Any kingdom divided against itself is laid waste; and any city or house divided against itself will not stand."

—Matthew 12:22–25

Jesus saw a blind man who couldn't speak and understood that a demon had caused the man's condition. Jesus healed the man and put his life back in order. When the people saw that this man could both see and speak, they began to wonder whether Jesus could be the Messiah. On the other hand, the Pharisees, the religious leaders of the day, raged against this healing. They didn't have to say anything; Jesus could see on their faces what they were thinking. At that moment Jesus began to speak about the kingdom in three ways.

He declared the kingdom as a federation

> *Knowing their thoughts Jesus said to them, "Any kingdom divided against itself is laid waste; and any city or house divided against itself will not stand. If Satan casts out Satan, he is divided against himself; how then shall his kingdom stand?"*

—Matthew 12:25–26

Jesus knew God's kingdom had a unified construction; it was singular in its purpose and intent. Jesus understood another important truth, as well: There are two distinct kingdoms, one of darkness and one of light. And they are both unified fronts.

> " There are two distinct kingdoms, one of darkness and one of light. And they are both unified fronts. "

It may help to imagine a boxing ring with two opponents. Two representatives of the two opposing kingdoms had stepped into the ring. In one corner was the kingdom of darkness represented by one central fallen angel, Satan. *Satan* is the New Testament term for the top position among the angels. He is the lead evil angel. In our day, we might say he's the head Soprano, the mob boss of the Cosmic Mafia. In his corner, he represents a kingdom of darkness, a united confederacy set on inflicting misery upon humanity.

> **"Darkness had fallen to the earth and taken humanity and the globe captive. Now Jesus had broken in to do battle ..."**

In the other corner was the kingdom of light represented by Jesus, the Christ, the Son of God who had come to earth. In everything he did and said, he represented God the Creator and his perfect, eternal plan. According to this plan, Jesus stepped out of heaven and onto the earth to verify heaven's message of ownership: "There is a new king in town."

The Scripture shows us that in Jesus' mind both kingdoms were distinct federations. Each had a united border focused intently on opposing purposes. One kingdom sought to expand the darkness; the other would reclaim the world by driving out that darkness with light.

Jesus' prayer was, "Thy kingdom come, thy will be done on earth as it is in heaven." He prayed this way because there were places on this earth where the kingdom of God had not yet been established. This would take place only when his work was completed on the cross. Until that time, the world would stay in the grip of darkness.

Jesus taught that we should pray for God's kingdom to continue to be established in this battle zone called the globe. When we pray in this way, we're specifically asking for God's kingdom to be established on this earth just as it is in heaven.

Jesus saw our world engaged in a real conflict affecting real people. Darkness had fallen to the earth and taken humanity and the globe captive. Now Jesus had broken in to do battle and to defeat the darkness and establish his kingdom of light. Jesus knew where misery comes from. He knew it came from the kingdom of darkness.

He defined the kingdom as a fight

"If I cast out demons by the Spirit of God, then the kingdom of God has come upon you. Or how can anyone enter the strong man's house and carry off his property, unless he first binds the strong man? And then he will plunder his house."

—Matthew 12:28–29

In these verses Jesus was illustrating the brawl between the two kingdoms. Satan, the strong man, had come to earth and taken humanity captive. He had entered in and taken possession of people through lies, addictions, destructive lifestyles, and deceptions. Now another had come who was able to bind the strong man. Jesus, the stronger man, broke into history to bind the kingdom of darkness and liberate the globe and its inhabitants.

Jesus defined the kingdom for us in both his words and his actions. He told a parable of a farmer who planted a crop of fine wheat only to have his enemy come at night and plant bags of weeds next to his good seed. When the seeds began to grow, the farmer knew he had a problem. What should he do, try and pick the weeds to minimize his loss? Jesus' answer defines the kingdom he saw. He said that the farmer should allow the two types of seed to grow in the field; the separation would take place during the harvest. Jesus was telling us that his kingdom was a theater of war.

The field represented his kingdom, and the good seed was the will of God planted to produce good fruit. The enemy who came by night represented Satan, who planted weeds to undo the good things God had planted in his kingdom. So two types of seed grew in the same ground. Their roots became entwined, yet they remained distinct and separate plants. The differences were in the purposes of the plants. The wheat would bear abundant fruit that would be used to grow more wheat. The only purpose of the weeds was to take up valuable space where wheat could have grown.

Jesus is teaching that two kingdoms fight for dominance over the same world. The conflict rages between his kingdom of light and the enemy's kingdom of darkness, both seeking victory over the cosmos. God will continue to plant only good things, while the enemy will do everything possible to uproot and destroy God's kingdom.

> **66 Jesus never required people to correct all their mistakes before they came to him. 99**

God's kingdom is all about advancing his creation. Satan's kingdom is all about bringing death, destruction, and de-creation to everything God initiates.

We've been planted in this field and this is where we keep trying to make sense out of our sufferings. We look at the weeds and we ask why bad things happen to us, because all we really want is to live a good and successful life.

Immediately following the tragic events of America's 9-11, the mainstream media interviewed leading spokespeople for Christianity. Each person was asked the same question, and each gave a similar answer.

The question: "How do you respond to the events of 9-11?"

The answer: "We don't know why God allowed this to happen."

The reality is God had nothing to do with that tragedy. He did not file the flight plan for those planes. The reason thousands died on that day was because several people willfully chose to carry out the destructive de-creating ambition of the enemy.

The pivot point of everything Jesus did was to advance his kingdom. When we understand this and then read the Gospels, we see that what appeared to be random acts of healing and short sermons were actually connected with Jesus' understanding of *the way things truly are*. He recognized that everything wrong in the world was an act of evil. When Jesus taught, he used objects like coins, sheep, bread, nets, and trees. When he encountered evidences of the presence of evil in the lives of people (the sick and crippled), he opposed the evil and restored them to health. Jesus came to set both the planet and the people free, and he did it without once cooperating or siding with evil.

Jesus came to fight. The stronger man came to take on the strong man, to bind him up and take his possessions, and to put humanity back into its rightful place. There was no question in Jesus' mind that he had come to do battle!

When we understand the fuller purpose Jesus came to accomplish, it changes the way we view our purpose on the earth and the way we carry out ministry. We will begin to see our role in the continued expansion of Christ's kingdom. Then, when we are faced with evil, we won't just sit down and take it.

> **" Jesus didn't come to just tell us stories and to make people feel better. Jesus came to do war! "**

Once this reality awakens within us, our worship suddenly has meaning, because through worship we are pushing back the darkness. When we study the Bible, we are pushing darkness out of our own lives. As we pour our lives into ministry through the church, we are joining forces with the armed forces of light. Now there is real drama—without the cape and gold boots! Now there is something of eternal substance to this life. Jesus didn't come to just tell us stories and to make people feel better. Jesus came to do war!

He demonstrated the kingdom in freedom

"If I cast out demons by the Spirit of God, then the kingdom of God has come upon you."

—Matthew 12:28

Jesus demonstrated

> 66 This truth does not describe a God of hate; it describes a God of infinite love who is by nature all good, all the time. 99

the purpose of his kingdom by liberating the crippled and lame man. Wherever Jesus traveled, he brought freedom, healing, salvation, forgiveness, and hope. I find it interesting that Jesus defined the success of his kingdom by the freedom people experienced, not by full churches. He did not base the success of his kingdom on how many people came to listen to him but by how many people experienced the freedom he came to deliver. The kingdom of God was demonstrated by freedom.

All the way through Jesus' ministry, freedom drives the plan. The kingdom is the backstory. Let me be very clear. It is precisely because God loves his creation and his people that he was willing to go to war to get it all back. This truth does not describe a God of hate; it describes a God of infinite love who is by nature all good, all the time. Ours is a God who has gone through the ultimate expense of sending his only Son to break into human history, to take on darkness, to defeat it on the cross, so that every one of us

> **Yes, bad things are going to happen to good people. But Christ came into this world because he was unwilling to put up with this situation.**

could experience true freedom.

So many in our world are trapped by addictions, held in bondage by the past, or confined by self-destructive lifestyles; they need Jesus' work of freedom. Yes, bad things are going to happen to good people. But Christ came into this world because he was unwilling to put up with this situation. Can we share in his non-tolerance?

Others need a work of forgiveness. They have such a history of failure that they doubt they could ever come to God after what they have done. However, Jesus never required people to correct all their mistakes before they came to him. Jesus told them to come just as they were.

Some of us need the kingdom of God to come and wash all the wrongs of our past out of us. We need deliverance, and we need to be rescued.

Many of us have been away from God for a long time. We claim it's because of churches, fears, bad experiences, and other unspoken things we won't talk about with anyone. The bottom line is that God has been at work to win us back into his presence so we can be fully free citizens in his kingdom.

Regardless of how bad a situation appears, perhaps now we can find the freedom of personal thought to choose the response that brings light into darkness, life into death, health into sickness. When faced with the bad things that are sure to come, perhaps now we can say with a deep, abiding conviction, "Yes, God *is* good, all the time."

Chapter Five

WHY DOESN'T GOD DO SOMETHING ABOUT IT?

In our culture today the significance of the cross has been reduced to something less than a piece of costume jewelry. It has become an ever-present symbol taking on the same importance as a good-luck charm or a token "tip of the hat" toward God. It's artsy, poetic, and cool to wear a cross. But originally the cross was a Roman tool of execution.

A quick glance at the popular music scene illustrates how little we understand the cross. In almost every pop, rock, or hip-hop video, the performers display crosses around their necks. Giant, diamond-encrusted crosses show off the artist's bling-bling. Yet Jesus didn't hang suspended between the earth and sky hoping that some day a rap-master would use the cross to signal the honeys that "his pockets be lined with plenty of ducketts." (Note to the non hip-hop reader: *Ducketts* is a term for money, a.k.a. *scrilla* and *grip*. Know what I'm sayin'?) Our cultural concept of the cross is, to say the least, a little bit crazy.

To Jesus, the cross was a weapon of war. Is that a new

> **"The cross killed criminals and innocents—and, not least, the Son of God."**

thought to you? We don't normally think of the cross as a weapon. However, it was never supposed to be a piece of jewelry with diamonds in it. And it definitely wasn't meant to be a love gift sent to you because you gave to some TV ministry. It was a killing device! It was gruesome because people were nailed to it. The cross killed criminals and innocents—and, not least, the Son of God. We've just lost sight of the significance and the meaning of the cross.

Jesus never lost sight of it. Early in his ministry, he knew there was a cross in his future. He knew he came to be the world's sacrifice. In fact, he knew the cross held the greatest possible significance for all of mankind; therefore, this symbol of death became Jesus' greatest weapon of warfare.

The high point of Jesus' earthly mission was his crucifixion, his final blow to the domain of darkness. It's impossible to understand the significance of the cross until we step back and see just how much it has affected human life. In the cross, God accomplished more than simply "doing something" about the evil, suffering, and pain in the world. He provided the way for us to find victory, relief, and comfort.

In Colossians 1:13–22, Paul wrote to believers who'd been taught that there were ways to become a Christian other than through Christ. They were told they should follow extreme laws that never appeared in the Scripture. That is, ungodly leaders made up rules and guidelines and used the religious system of the day to enforce their own agendas. The apostle Paul told them the only thing that would impact their lives and give them the freedom they sought was to receive Jesus as he is and embrace what he did on the cross. He showed them three ways the cross was a weapon of warfare.

The cross ended the cosmic war

This is precisely how the writers of the New Testament spoke of the cross. Most of us have never recognized this truth. Our understanding of the cross begins and ends with its benefit to us. We only think of the cross in terms of what it does for us. We've learned that if we were the only persons on the earth Jesus would have died just for us. And he would have—but the effect on the cosmos would have been the same.

> *He rescued us from the domain of darkness, and*
> *transferred us to the kingdom of His beloved Son.*
>
> —Colossians 1:13

The domain of darkness existed in, and had legal control over, the world. The Scripture teaches that before time existed, Satan opposed God's initiative and sought to advance his own ambition. Satan approached God

> 66 We only think of the cross in terms of what it does for *us*. 99

and put Him on notice: *"I* will be God!" God met Satan's challenge. In the great heavenly battle that followed, Satan and his Cosmic Mafia were defeated and banished from heaven to roam the earth as eternal exiles of heaven. In this way the world became the test tube of Satan's ambitions.

God placed Adam and Eve in the garden to be his legal caretakers of creation. He told them to grow the garden and multiply to fill the earth. He had created Adam and Eve and all their descendents to be the legal caretakers of the globe.

The Scripture continues. Satan came into the garden and spoke with Adam and Eve, convincing them to give up their legal standing as earth's caretakers. He told them that if they simply did what they chose to do rather than what God told them to do, they would not die. Instead, they would become like God. (This must have been similar to the lie he had told the angels who had decided to join him in his attempt to overthrow heaven.)

In the moment Adam and Eve chose to forfeit their legal standing as stewards of the earth, Satan became lord of the earth. He didn't steal it; Adam and Eve chose to give it away. From that moment on, the enemy held both the globe and humanity under his control. Everyone born after that moment came under the influence of the one who sought to de-create everything God had created. As a result, everything we struggle with today is a consequence of the ambition of the evil one.

There is a pattern of thought that will help us understand how the life and death of Christ truly affected the entire cosmos. At just the right time, God entered this world by being born as a baby. Mary had become pregnant by the Holy Spirit. Although Mary and Joseph were legally married, they had not had sexual relations. Jesus had no earthly father; God was his father. There never had been, nor will there ever be, anyone born like he was. Jesus came out of heaven to the earth where his enemy had fallen.

He was not born a captive child of the darkness. He was born a free man, the second Adam, the key to God's plan to take back his creation. Jesus grew up pure, untouched, and unscathed by sin. At the right time he went public with his ministry. Firmly planted in his mind was the completion of his mission to defeat darkness. He knew that one day his life would end on the cross.

During the twenty-four hours before his crucifixion, Jesus stood before religious and governmental officials who sentenced him to die. In Matthew 27, we read about Jesus being nailed to the cross. His was a legal execution that had been properly sentenced. In fact, everything Jesus did was legal, so I believe he had to legally win back the world. Jesus could not just take it back; he had no legal claim to it. Satan held the title on the cosmos. It had to be won back legally.

> 66 If we reduce the role of the cross to simply what it did for our sin, we miss the greater impact of the cross upon evil. 99

When Jesus hung on the cross, the environment changed drastically. The Bible says the sky went black as dark, and light battled over the Son of God. No doubt Satan thought his plan was working out. He had nailed the Son of God to the cross and was certain of winning. He had successfully manipulated Judas to sell out Jesus, and now the Lamb of God hung on a killing post. Finally, darkness covered the sky! He had won. He had maintained his grip on his title to the cosmos. However …

> *[The Father] rescued us from the domain of darkness,*
> *and transferred us to the kingdom of His beloved Son.*
>
> —Colossians 1:13

God had used the enemy's desire against him. As darkness covered the site of the crucifixion, Jesus cried out, "It is finished!" In that moment the Bible says graves opened up and bodies popped out of the ground. An unmistakable shift was transforming the universe.

The cross was not just about taking care of our personal sin; it was about the *reclaiming of the entire globe.* If we reduce the role of the cross to simply what it did for our sin, we miss the greater impact of the cross upon evil.

> **❝ I have heard tons of preachers get up and yell about this: 'Jesus is seated at the right hand of God! Amen, bless God! Let's go eat!' ❞**

Evil had literally ravaged the entire universe. When Jesus was on the cross, he was winning back that universe. He was taking the lordship of the earth away from the enemy and reclaiming it for himself.

When he said "It is finished!" he meant more than the forgiveness of our sin. He meant that he had accomplished his purpose for being on the earth. He had won back the earth. He now held the title for all existence in his hand. Jesus' death on the cross was a total victory—all creation reclaimed on behalf of the light. This is what makes it possible for our sins to be removed and for us to have the life of God come to live within us. Salvation, forgiveness, and new life all took place because of this shift of ownership. The death of Jesus Christ on the cross ended the cosmic war that began before time. God got his world back.

We need to take a step back and understand what we are offering to people when we talk with them about the life Jesus offers. The death of Jesus liberated the world and stripped Satan of his hold on mankind. He destroyed the enemy and disarmed him of his power. He made a way for people to break ranks with darkness and side up with the kingdom of light. The cross ended the cosmic war.

The cross empowered Christians to win every day

He is also head of the body, the church; and He is the beginning, the firstborn from the dead, so that He Himself will come to have first place in everything.

—Colossians 1:18

Paul now shifts to show how the cross personally affects us. When Jesus died on the cross, he stripped the legal hold that the enemy had over the world and broke the controlling power that he had over people; however, he did not do away with the enemy. Nowhere does the Bible say that Jesus made the enemy disappear. Even while Jesus was dying on the cross, evil was still on the earth and still remains to this day.

This year, the University of Oklahoma beat Texas in football, but Texas is still there. OU's win over Texas didn't break the state off of our continent and make it disappear; Texas is still there. In the same way, the legal hold the enemy held over the universe was taken from him, but his presence remains on the earth. True, the enemy has been mortally wounded, and his power has been taken from him. Now all he can do is make suggestions and try to instigate stress and havoc in our lives.

> 66 Wherever evil rears its ugly head, our job is to fight it. Are you beginning to see it? 99

The cross empowers us to win our battles with the enemy. God's plan is for believers to daily claim the victory Jesus won for us on the cross. God's plan has always been for believers to take this victory and live it out, enforcing it through every spectrum of life. Wherever evil rears its ugly head, our job is to fight it. Are you beginning to see it? Our life in

Christ has greater weight and purpose for this planet than we ever dreamed possible. The cross has equipped us to take on evil … and to win!

The cross didn't set us free so we could feel happy and sing nice little songs. Jesus' death set us free so we could extend his win at Golgotha throughout creation. Each generation of believers is responsible to live the victory that is theirs on the cross. This means that we begin to offer to the world complete forgiveness, true freedom, eternal hope, perfect love, and healing for the body, soul, and spirit. Those of us who willingly give our lives to Christ, and ask him to be the leader of our lives, become the beneficiaries of these things. God leaves us here to begin to live throughout the earth what was won for us on the cross.

Talk about radical Christianity—this is it! This type of living goes way beyond just wearing a necklace or singing a song. Our freedom has function. We proclaim the presence of God and literally remove evil from this earth through the lives we live. As we pray, speak, and live together, we demonstrate to others what was won on the cross. Do you see it? We're equipped to win.

The cross exalted Christ over the world

So that He Himself will come to have first place in everything.

—Colossians 1:18

Jesus has first place in this world, but it is only played out through the lives of his people. If the world sees a weak Jesus, it's because they see defeated and weak Christians. Society will be turned around only when believers begin to enforce the work of the cross in their lives. Politics will change when believers begin to put these victories into effect as they work in the political arena. When we understand and live out what was won on the cross for us, marriages will heal, addictions will give way, and hope will come shining through again. In the simplest language, our goal is for Christ to have first place in everything we do.

Christ owns everything because of his victory on the cross. He has been exalted over this entire world. He has become the firstborn among men. He was placed on a cross, then in a tomb, and then he ascended to heaven and is even now seated at the right hand of God. I have heard tons of preachers get up and yell about this: "Jesus is seated at the right hand of God! Amen, bless God! Let's go eat!" I always wondered why this was such a big deal. What does it have to do with anything? Well, Paul answers this question when he writes in Romans:

> *Who will bring a charge against God's elect? God is the one who justifies; who is the one who condemns? Christ Jesus is He who died, yes, rather who was raised, who is at the right hand of God, who also intercedes for us.*
>
> —Romans 8:33–34

I talk with people every day who feel condemned and overwhelmed by defeat. Many of them can't pinpoint where the feelings come from. They know they are Christians, but they have powerful feelings of failure and worthlessness. They feel they stand before God accused and condemned.

Before Jesus defeated darkness on the cross, the enemy had access into the presence of God. "Then he showed me Joshua the high priest standing before the angel of the LORD, and Satan standing at his right hand to accuse him" (Zech. 3:1). The right hand of God is the place where Satan would stand and accuse believers (remember how it happened in the Book of Job).

But because of his victory on the cross, God has installed Jesus to be seated at his right hand! "The LORD says to my Lord: 'Sit at My right hand until I make Your enemies a footstool for Your feet'" (Ps. 110:1). This means the enemy no longer has access to the right hand of God. Jesus, the victor, is not *standing* there, not waiting to gain that position. No, he's *seated* there, permanently holding this position. "He is the one whom God exalted to His right hand as a Prince and a Savior, to grant repentance to Israel, and forgiveness of sins" (Acts 5:31). Christ's presence there makes every person who is in him uncondemnable, untouchable. In Colossians 2, Paul summarizes what Jesus did with his death on the cross:

Having canceled out the certificate of debt consisting of decrees against us, which was hostile to us; and He has taken it out of the way, having nailed it to the cross. When He had disarmed the rulers and authorities, He

*made a public display of them, having triumphed over
them through Him.*

—Colossians 2:14–15

Jesus has removed the accuser and broken his hold.
Everything we have done against ourselves, God, and others
has been cancelled.

Now your debt is cancelled

No matter how much or how often we have sinned, Jesus'
victory over darkness and death has cancelled out our certificate of debt. Let me illustrate this with a little story.

When it comes to driving, I'd rather not go too slow. In
fact, the fish symbol on my car is magnetic, so I can take it
off when I need to drive fast. (You should never let those fish
get in the way of your driving habits!)

Years ago I was driving through Alabama and got stopped
for speeding. When the officer pulled me over, I was on my
best behavior. I kept both hands on the wheel like a good
driver should. The officer approached the car and said, "Do
you know why I stopped you? You were going 100 miles per
hour." I thought to myself, *Really? That's all? You should have
stopped me earlier, because a few miles back I was really flying.*

He went through the entire procedure of getting my
license and began lecturing me while writing a ticket for several hundred dollars. Now I have firsthand evidence that the
slogan of Alabama is: "He's different; let's get him!"

I was frightened, not from hearing his lecture about the
dangers of driving at high rates of speed, but because he held

the power to take both me and my license to jail. After he drove off, I thought of all of the things I wished I had said—

- When he asked, "Do you know why I stopped you?" I wish I'd said, "Because you ran out of doughnuts?"
- When he asked, "Did you know that you were speeding?" I wish I'd said, "You had to catch up with me, didn't you?"
- When he asked, "Can I see your license?" I wish I would have been quick enough to come back with, "Only if I can shoot your gun."

The officer handed me my ticket and said, "If you take this to the courthouse, you can get it taken off of your record." I had the time, so I went down to the courthouse (a completely different level of hell from the one I experienced at the side of the highway) and anxiously waited in line to take care of my ticket.

Finally, it was my turn. I handed my sweat-soaked ticket to a lady with a big beehive hairdo that had several pencils sticking out of it. There must have been two cans of hairspray holding up her "do." (Just over her right shoulder was a "Danger – Flammable!" sign with an arrow pointing to her head.) She just kept looking at me through her horn-rimmed glasses. I handed her the ticket. "I was told you could take care of this for me," I said.

She took the ticket, stamped it, and tossed it in a basket. Reaching for another piece of paper, she handed me the

> **The enemy no longer has access to the right hand of God. We are no longer accused for the wrong things we do. Jesus sits at God's right hand praying for us and encouraging us.**

receipt and said, "You're done. You can go." I stuck the receipt in my pocket and walked out to my car.

By the time I got back to my car, I had started to calm down quite a bit. I pulled the receipt out of my pocket. Across the paper, hairdo lady had stamped "Cancelled." I didn't owe anything.

This is exactly what the cross did—cancelled our sin-debt. What we could never do on our own, Jesus did on the cross. He won back his creation and stripped the enemy of his legal hold over the world. He settled the cosmic score between God and Satan, once and for all. The enemy no longer has access to the right hand of God. We are no longer accused for the wrong things we do. Jesus sits at God's right hand praying for us and encouraging us. And all this, after he had won the eternal battle for first place in the universe.

Those who will ask God to step into their lives become the beneficiaries of his life, freedom, forgiveness, healing, goodness, and his hope. These gifts are all available to us because of the score that was settled for us on the cross.

In the middle of everyday problems, we can be sure that

nothing is able to separate us from the love and personal attention of God. Jesus' victory guarantees the eternal presence of his kingdom in and on our lives.

So why do bad things happen? Let's be clear. Bad things happen because there is an opposing ambition that seeks to destroy God's initiative. These things I'm saying about good and evil are living truths that can directly impact our lives. God designed his plan to recover the world so that we could experience victory over every form of evil and temptation, day by day.

When facing evil, we can be certain of three truths. First, the evil, or the bad thing, did not originate from God. Second, regardless of how long the evil sticks around, we can trust him for the duration. Third, God remains in constant control.

Let it sink into your heart

These aren't just truths to know; they are truths to live by. A few months ago I knew something wasn't right with my health. I was tired all the time, and I had large, black circles under my eyes. One night after I had spoken in Oklahoma City, a doctor friend of mine said, "Dave, you don't look right. How do you feel?" I told him I'd been "low energy" for several weeks, and he said that he needed to do some blood work on me.

Early the next morning he came by my house and woke me up to draw blood. I was still in my robe when I sat down in my study. I never opened my eyes; I just held out my arm and said, "Here, take it." He wrapped that stretchy thing around my elbow, thumped my arm a couple of times, and stuck me with the nnnneeedle ... (I really hate those pointy things. I feel queasy right now. I should take a break.)

Okay, anyway. He took my blood to his office and ran tests, and I went back to bed. A couple of days went by, and my mind began to weave an intricate tapestry picturing all sorts of things that could be wrong with me. I was worried and afraid. Finally, he called and told me exactly what was wrong and what I needed to do to correct the imbalances he found in my blood.

When I hung up the phone, the truths of this book saturated my soul. I was still emotional, but I didn't derail on God. I knew this bad thing had not come from him. I was comfortable knowing that regardless of how long this bad blood balance hung around, I could make it through—because there is nothing that can separate me from God's abiding presence. I had a sense that regardless of how things turned out, God was still acting on my behalf, and I could trust him. These truths had moved from my head to my heart and could now direct the way I chose to respond to my situation.

And that's the point: The time has come to make the power of these realities of the cross *a functioning part of our lives*. Every generation of believers has the God-given responsibility to embody the completed reality of the cross. We are called to be more than shining lights in the darkness. When we are reclaimed by Christ, we are literally appointed to personify the realities of the shift in cosmic ownership brought about by the cross. Our lives have a purpose and meaning far greater than we ever thought. Believers are in a position to have the greatest impact on the influence of evil in our world. We are the body of Christ, and we regulate

> **Our lives have a purpose and meaning far greater than we ever thought.**

the effects of the cross in this world by choosing to live in agreement with the completed realities of the cross.

But that's where it always seems the most difficult. How do we transfer the words of this book into the story of our lives? When we're actually faced with evil, how can we be sure this stuff works? That's the next subject coming your way.

Chapter Six

How am I going to get through this?

I f we're not careful, we might be tempted to reduce Jesus to a painting, a postcard, or a bedtime story for children. We forget that this is a king who came to do war. He came to set up his kingdom in the cosmos. Jesus came to do combat with the enemy ... and win!

Because of this, Jesus saw every disease as an act of war waged by the enemy. In effect, Jesus healed people as an act of counter-terrorism. Everything he did demonstrated that his kingdom was in the process of overthrowing the kingdom of darkness. We must not lose sight of this.

The intent of this book is to help us recapture Jesus' combat mentality. This way of thinking will help us learn how to live in this world and not give up. Without the mind of Christ, we'll soon develop combat fatigue.

It's easy to see how the church has drifted away from this way of thinking by looking at the battles churches have chosen to fight. Years ago it was Ouija boards. Every minister opposed them, saying, "If you use one, you'll end up sacrificing your cat to Satan!" How dumb is that? The only thing a Ouija board shows is that Satan is a slow speller! If that's the fastest the king of darkness can spell, he's a lamebrain!

Then it was rock-n-roll. I know you're not going to believe me, but way back before CDs there were these black round discs called records, which came in albums. (You can see these discs being used in rap videos today, but back then there were actually songs on them, not just scratching noises.) For a time, some people made a big deal about records supposedly having evil messages on them—called back-masking—which you could hear when you played records backward. So certain evangelists would haul turntables into churches and play every great rock-n-roll album in the country to show the evil backward messages hidden on them. They would say, "When this record is played backward, it has the whole satanic Bible on it, *listen!*" They'd play it backward, and it sounded like Kermit the Frog belching after too many chips with salsa.

I would always raise my hand and say, "I'm not hearing what you are hearing." Every recorded message they played backward was supposed to be really evil, like: "Kill your family!" I always wondered why they never seemed to contain helpful messages like, "Clean up your room!"

Then, instead of playing the records to audiences, these preachers just shifted to burning the records. I attended weekend retreats and summer camps where kids would burn whole albums. I stood by and thought: *Give them to me; I'll take care of them. Don't burn the Eagles!*

Then, just a few years ago, religious people started attacking Teletubbies. "Teletubbies are wrong because one of them is gay!" I was watching the news when this was reported and thought, *Huh? Teletubbies don't even have genitals. They have TVs in their tummies!* Perhaps the creators of *Teletubbies* should come back with a new character to add to their lineup. They could have a masculine Teletubbie that always watches WWF and monster truck pulls.

Every time I turn around, they're boycotting something. Recently it was Harry Potter. The report is that the books and movies are satanic and loaded with the occult. People are forming organizations to ban Harry from their community bookstores and theaters. I was at the mall and heard a mom telling her kid, "Harry Potter is evil and just make-believe, anyway; you can't go see it! We're going to go see Santa."

Then it was video games. The claim was, "They cause our kids to be violent!" I'm not aware of anyone being possessed by the spirit of Super Mario Brothers.

The most recent religious outcry is, "What would Jesus drive?" Apparently these activists believe Jesus would

> "Jesus would drive a Hummer, and I don't mean one of those yellow SpongeBob H-2s. He would drive the real Hummer; the one that says, 'I'm rollin' into town and my kingdom's takin' over!'"

drive a Kia or an electric car instead of an SUV. Let's be clear—if you're carrying around twelve other guys (plus fishing gear) everywhere you go, then a Yugo really isn't an option.

And really, is gasoline a problem for Jesus? After all, he lived in the Middle East, the epicenter of petroleum. And besides, anybody who could turn water into wine certainly could keep his tank topped off. And that Middle East rough terrain demands a rugged 4X4. So, in my humble opinion, I would say that Jesus would drive a Hummer, and I don't mean one of those yellow SpongeBob H-2s. He would drive the real Hummer; the one that says, "I'm rollin' into town and my kingdom's takin' over!" Put yourself in his place. Jesus needed something he could stand on top of to teach the crowd that had gathered. Now I ask you, how would Jesus look giving the Sermon on the Mount standing on the roof of a minivan?

These boycotts show us that the church has lost sight of the greater battle. We live in the middle of a full-scale world-wide conflict. We have either never realized the multidimensional size of this battle, or we have chosen to invest our energies in fighting fringe struggles that really have little to do with the frontline of the war. Fighting the symptoms may provide temporary relief, but the virus remains. Our efforts should focus on the greater battle being waged in the cosmos. Remember: "Our struggle is not against flesh and blood" (Eph. 6:12).

Our struggle is not against movies, clothing, popular music, or culture. The people on TV fronting Christianity's stance against these things are the same people making Christians look ignorant and out of touch. And many of us not only allow it, we endorse their ranting.

When Paul writes his letter to the Ephesians, he's preparing that church to recapture its view of the greater battle. He tells them how they are to live in this world in light of it. The Book of Ephesians deals with the subjects of the family, our individual conduct, and the value of personal honor. The content of Paul's letter equips people to live decisively godly and practical lives.

He cuts to the point where he says, "Our battle is not against all that *stuff.*" In Ephesians 6:10 and following, Paul explains how we can live with the proper warfare mentality, even when everything in life seems to be headed in the wrong direction. Paul is saying, "This is how we are to live in the midst of it."

It's unavoidable; we will face suffering and evil in our lives. We could succumb to fate, passivity, or anger. Or, we can live according to the truth that evil was defeated on the cross. The challenge then becomes making this principle practical in our lives. This means more than simply accepting a truth. It will require personal action in three areas of life.

We must remove the areas of weakness from our lives

Any time we face resistance, we must remember that the condition of our lives has a supernatural impact on the circumstances we are facing.

Finally, be strong in the Lord and in the strength of His might. Put on the full armor of God, so that you will be able to stand firm against the schemes of the devil.

—Ephesians 6:10–11

The word *finally* is a call to action. Paul is calling us to act, because we are not spectators in the spiritual battle. Our prayers, for example, literally place God's hands into our situation.

The word *schemes* can refer to "footholds." It means that the enemy tries to get leverage in our lives. Our enemy levels personal attacks against each of us at the point of our weaknesses. He schemes to work his way into our thought life, our appetites, our addictions, our instincts. His aim is to gain a place of control. That's why, when we come to pray over someone else's life or over some other major situation, we first need to remove the areas of weakness from our own lives. Paul is saying to us, "Make certain there is no foothold in your life that the enemy can use to mess with you. Don't let the enemy find your weaknesses."

> 66 Fear is always debilitating. Fear eats faith. 99

Any time we go to battle, we must always remove the areas of weakness in all of our lives. Our weaknesses become visible in three major areas:

Unbelief Suppose you're facing evil and praying that God will fight on your behalf. At the same time do you maintain thoughts like: "What's the use?" Our unbelief sabotages the effectiveness of prayer. We must continually reject every ounce of unbelief that we may be feeling or thinking. This is an ongoing process. Simply because we have renounced unbelief once does not make us immune to the continuous undermining effects of unbelief.

But be encouraged here too. Jesus said: "If you have faith the size of a mustard seed, you will say to this mountain, 'Move from here to there,' and it will move" (Matt. 17:20). So don't feel you have to brainwash yourself in some way or have a faith as big as the mountains. A mustard seed is quite tiny, isn't it? Just keep your focus on the bigness of God.

Fear Fear is always debilitating. Fear eats faith and cannot coexist with faith. Anytime the enemy uses fear to try and steal the confidence we have in God, he makes us withdraw from the fight, pull away from the challenge, and think we can't do that thing God says we can do. The enemy knows that if he can make us fearful, then we won't fight.

Sin Anything that keeps us from experiencing the full presence of God is sin. The difficulty for most of us is not choosing between the clearly good and obviously bad things in life. The hard choices are more subtle. Sometimes we're even lured by the advice of friends who themselves have fallen into sin.

When I pray for a friend or a troubling situation, even before I get ready to speak, I run a check on these three areas of my life. I make sure that I say, "God, to the best of my ability, I reject every unbelieving thought, every ounce of fear I may have at this moment, and I reject the vices in my life. I reject the areas where I've been duped before, I renounce the things I've said that shouldn't have been said, and the things I've done that I wish I could take back. God, I turn away from those things, and I open my life fully to you right now."

When we pray like this, we begin to put ourselves in a position of fighting in strength. As citizens of heaven we are under a code; we can't fight the battles we are called to fight when our lives have been leveraged. If we are going to fight like Jesus, we have to remove every area of weakness so the enemy can't set up a control center within us.

We must recognize the arenas of spiritual warfare

For our struggle is not against flesh and blood, but against the rulers, against the powers, against the world forces of this darkness, against the spiritual forces of wickedness in the heavenly places.

—Ephesians 6:12

Paul is saying to the Ephesians, "I know about the pagan worship in your city; I know about all the madness that is going on; I know about the astrology." (Astrology. That's another boycott I didn't mention earlier. "You must stay away from Ms. Cleo!" Before her it was Dionne Warwick and the Psychic Friend Network that, as you already know, went bankrupt. You'd think that if they were true psychics, they'd have seen that bankruptcy coming ... . Maybe the only thing you can be sure of with psychics is their ability to operate a neon sign.) Paul is telling us that we are not on earth to oppose everything that we disagree with. He's telling us to recognize in which arena the war is being fought. It's one of these—

Within the cosmos Almost everyone in the New Testament believed that there was a real world positioned between the earth and the heavenly places. This was the place where supernatural beings fought. Paul simply mentioned the existence of this world when he wrote that our struggle is against spiritual forces in heavenly places. The people of his day accepted this as fact and knew that the cosmos could not be seen with human eyes but required spiritual awareness.

Upon the earth There are battles taking place all over the earth. Some battles extend over small towns. Others center over capitals, cities, and even entire nations. If you travel like I do, you can feel it. I sense a pronounced spirit of racism whenever my plane lands in Memphis. The city is divided in half: On the western side of Memphis, most residents are one skin color; on the east side

66 I'm not trying to be creepy or spooky, but I believe de-creating forces reside in cities throughout the world. 99

they're another skin color. In my opinion, this segregation isn't just the result of any specific political agenda or socioeconomic phenomenon. It's spiritual in nature.

I'm not trying to be creepy or spooky, but I believe de-creating forces reside in cities throughout the world. There is a reason that outside our country we find so much poverty and sickness—and it has little to do with our nation's wealth and medical knowledge. Spirits hold sway over those lands—spirits of poverty and spirits of sickness. I'm not saying evil spirits lurk behind everything bad, so don't look for the evil spirit making your car run out of gas. (You're sitting on the side of the road simply because you chose not to stop at the gas station.) I'm just saying that changing a country's economy requires much more than putting the right person in office. Healing a country from devastating disease requires more than politics. De-creating spirits are influencing people in authority with an evil power.

Paul wants us to understand that this war is much larger than the way people look and what they do. A war rages in the cosmos and upon this earth.

In people's lives Each of us fights our own private wars. Some of these wars are more severe than others. Some of us fight lifestyle wars, others fight wars affecting our instincts, and still others fight wars centering on personal appetites. Each of these wars is spiritual in nature. Paul wakes us up by saying, "Everything I have told you up to this point about your families, your conduct, and your life on this earth is spiritual. Every moral and spiritual decision is based inside one of these three arenas."

Many times natural disasters are a result of a cosmic war: mudslides in Mexico or California, earthquakes around the world, raging forest fires. These are very real disasters with sometimes supernatural causes. It is important to understand that God is not initiating these things. We simply need to be able to identify the arenas of war.

Here are some facts to keep in mind about the enemy's strategy: (1) There is an ongoing, intensifying large-scale battle. The virus of the evil one has saturated this earth. The Cosmic Mafia has set up its game throughout the world, and its influence is pervasive. (2) The war has been organized for maximum destruction, with rulers and powers and forces in heavenly places. Everything God seeks to do, this evil seeks to undo. (3) The rebellion seeks to carry out the ambition of evil. Therefore, before we start blaming God, we must step back and remember, "An evil spiritual force is driving all of this." Paul is calling us to be engaged in fighting this war. It's not a conservative or liberal war, a republican or democratic war, a color war, or an economic war. It's not a war to end Muslim terrorism around the world, or a war to end hunger for all of mankind. It is at base a spiritual war. And whether or not we know it, or admit it, we are in the big middle of it.

When our lives are attacked, we must recognize that these assaults originate from a spiritual power and that the enemy is trying to bring havoc into our lives. These attacks do not preclude our choice of responses. Rather, they should remind us of the various options we have available to us in Christ.

In my travels, I meet couples whose marriages have been ripped apart, with some having had their relationships with their kids disintegrate almost into nothing. They are angry at each other, and it has yet to cross their minds that any of their difficulties might be spiritual. Everything to them has become personal. Like many of us, they face the bad times with nothing more than their own abilities to endure. Yet that will to survive has already been heavily taxed beyond repair. You see, the ambition of evil is too strong for us to face on our own. Until we learn to look beyond our finite power, we will never have the ability to launch an offensive.

We must resolutely attack all wickedness

Paul says we must fight the proper war. A lot of secondary skirmishes go on all around us, but Paul reminds us to fight the right war. We have to step into the right arena and fight wickedness and evil whenever it makes its presence known. But, how do you do this with resolve?

> *Therefore, take up the full armor of God, so that you will be able to resist in the evil day, and having done everything, to stand firm.*
>
> —Ephesians 6:13

Throughout Ephesians 6:13–17, Paul talks about how the full spiritual armor works in our lives. Lots of people have taken this concept and made it into a little devotional act involving putting on the various pieces of armor. But this misses the true intent of Scripture. Reference to the armor points to *what we already carry in our spirit.* The armor was given to us when we opened our lives to Christ. We don't put the armor on or take it off; instead, we're called to activate what we already have.

The *helmet of salvation* is the confidence we have that our standing in Christ is secure. Nothing can separate us from the life God placed in us. The *breastplate of righteousness* is what Christ has done in us. He has declared us to be righteous and pure. Because of the new covenant, we have a new standing and a new status. The *belt of truth* guards us from any desire that could pull us away from God or possibly lead us to a place that would break the heart of God. The *shield of faith* is the assurance that God is always good. Even when the enemy attacks and arrows are fired, we take shelter behind the truth that God is good and that he loves his kids. The attacks do not come from him; he is our shield in the midst of the battle. We live our lives in Christ with this armor already in place.

The fact that our feet are covered with the *gospel* is the knowledge that we carry the life of God into every situation. We carry with us the message of the kingdom, that there is a life greater than physical life. Jesus came to deposit in humankind his eternal life. This is what we carry with us as we walk into life.

The *sword of the Spirit* is the Word of God. We use the truth that is God's Word to fight every lie leveled against us by the evil one. Every lie fired into our life has an equal truth to disarm it. The more we interact with God's Word and allow it to wash over us, renewing our minds, the more wisdom and truth we carry with us. The truths we experientially know about the Bible become our arsenal to fight with.

Paul ends this portion of his letter by saying that we are to pray at all times. This means we are to stay in step with the life of God. Regardless of where we live or what our daily tasks include, prayer is our channel of communication to help us stay in sync with God's presence.

> **You may not be fighting a battle right now, but that doesn't mean there aren't battles going on around you.**

We've been equipped with everything Paul has described. We need to put it into action in our daily circumstances. To ignore our armor is to remain vulnerable to the enemy's ambition. Activate the whole armor of God that has been attached to your spirit. Don't ignore the very thing God has given you to guard you from the enemy's attack: "and having done everything, to stand firm" (Eph. 6:13).

Simply put, make certain that everything you do strengthens your stand against evil. Here are three ways to maintain a firm stand:

Connect to the community No one stands alone. Paul calls the entire community to be present. One of my greatest concerns speaking in Bible studies all across the country is the number of people who come and go, who are not really connected to the community of Christ. The will of God is that we would not go it alone in our battles. Through local churches we connect to an army of people fighting together. If we feel we're alone, we must remember that somewhere there's a community we need to join. That community needs us as much as we need them.

Be alert to the hurt You may not be fighting a battle right now, but that doesn't mean there aren't battles going on around you. We need to be alert to people under attack; we need to pray for them and encourage them. That's why verse 18 says we should pray at all times in the Spirit. See the hurting people around you, and extend a helping hand.

Pray your way through We can spend our prayer time asking God why things happen the way they do. But that's not how to pray your way through. We pray through when we realize that prayer actually has the power to change any situation on earth by bringing heaven and earth into agreement.

> *"I will give you the keys of the kingdom of heaven;*
> *and whatever you bind on earth shall have been bound in*
> *heaven, and whatever you loose on earth shall have been*
> *loosed in heaven."*
>
> —Matthew 16:19

In Jesus we have the power of binding and loosing. When we face the ambition of the enemy, we simply need to engage the situation in prayer. There's nothing we can do ourselves to change that situation except use the keys Jesus has given us ... and pray! Jesus is the only one who holds the legal rights to bring about change on the earth. He's seated at God's right hand, and he has the power of heaven at his disposal. Praying our way through evil means that we identify the specific situation and literally bind its growth while releasing the power of Christ's kingdom to take its place. Prayer is powerful; it changes the earth. In prayer we set up heaven's boundaries on the earth, and inside these boundaries the power of the kingdom runs free.

Bring your kingdom, Lord!

What you've just read is the New Testament understanding of evil and suffering in our world. The concepts in this book give us the ability to take a long look at the world and be unflinchingly honest about what we see. Real Christianity never glosses things over with simple answers; instead, it acknowledges a real battle with a real enemy and real casualties. An all-good God fights the evil ambition in order to advance his

> " Prayer is powerful; it changes the earth. In prayer we set up heaven's boundaries on the earth, and inside these boundaries the power of the kingdom runs free. "

kingdom in the midst of suffering.

God didn't create or cause evil. Evil was born out of the heart of one created being who took it upon himself to de-create everything the Creator

> 66 God's plan today is the same as it was when he defeated Satan and exiled him from heaven. 99

created. Christ invaded the world and legally took control of the world away from Satan. On the cross he provided everything necessary for us not only to survive any situation but to conquer it.

God's plan today is the same as it was when he defeated Satan and exiled him from heaven. It is the prayer that Jesus prayed when his disciples said, "Lord, teach us to pray." God's plan for the world, and his plan for us, shines through in fourteen wonderful words that should be our prayer every day:

> *Thy kingdom come,*
> *thy will be done;*
> *on earth as it is in heaven.*

Readers' Guide

*For Personal Reflection
or Group Discussion*

Introduction to
the Readers' Guide

The Questions for Life series gets to the heart of what we believe. Sometimes life just doesn't seem fair! *Why Is This Happening to Me?* is a question that crosses everyone's mind at some point in life. As you read through this book, use the discussion points in the following pages to take you to another level. You can study these points on your own or invite a friend or a group of friends to go through the book with you.

Whether you are just checking God out or desiring to go deeper in your relationship with him, let yourself be challenged to change the way you live based on the answers you discover to life's most pressing questions.

Chapter 1: Why do bad things happen to good people?

1. Think about the original Christmas and our modern depictions of it. In your opinion, how different are they?

2. How is our societal view of evil different from what the Bible actually teaches?

3. What impact do our choices have on the kingdom of God? When have you seen this principle in action?

4. How is the Christmas story in the Book of Revelation like, and unlike, the story in the Gospels?

5. What role does the church play in Jesus' ministry? Is this what you expected, or is it radical? Why?

6. What is your own answer to the question of this chapter's title? What new insights have you gained through your reading?

7. Where does the question most specifically apply in your life these days?

Chapter 2: God, where are you?

1. When have you been most concerned about God's whereabouts (or existence)? Why?

2. What kind of theology do religious bumper stickers teach? Is this positive? Why or why not?

3. How does Jesus' view of Satan differ from our typical cartoon image of him?

4. What are some ways you see evil at work around you?

5. What did Jesus believe about the source of evil? How did he respond to it?

6. Why is it so important to have the presence of Christ living in you? What happens if he does not?

7. What is the next step you'd like to take in order to apply the truths of this chapter to your life?

Chapter 3: Is God trying to teach me something through this?

1. Some of us construct our theology from random, disconnected phrases that we have pieced together over the years. What are the benefits of this approach? What harm can it cause?

2. When have you felt that God was trying to teach you something through a painful circumstance? How did you respond? How did things turn out?

3. In what ways have you seen the enemy attack the will of God in your life?

4. What kind of distinction did Jesus make when dealing with hurting people in the Gospels? Do we often make this same distinction?

5. In what ways do our expectations affect our actual church experience? When has this been most obvious to you, personally?

6. Do you take hell seriously? Why, or why not?

Chapter 4: How good is God, really?

1. Name some of the discrepancies between what we say about God in church on Sundays and what we really believe the rest of the week. Which one is the most important to you?

2. In what ways does our society pass judgment on God? Can you give an example?

3. Do you think there are exceptions to God's goodness? Why, or why not?

4. What are the two kingdoms that are at war? What is each of these kingdoms trying to accomplish?

5. How does this warfare mentality affect our worship? Talk about a time when you noticed this.

6. In what areas of your life do you need to experience freedom? How could other members of your group help with this?

Chapter 5: Why doesn't God do something about it?

1. How have you noticed people using the cross? How does our use of the cross often reduce its significance and impact in our culture?

2. What are some of the benefits we receive from the cross?

3. Was the cross only for our sin? If not, what else was it for?

4. What are some ways we can extend the "win" of the cross into the world? Into your own life, in practical ways?

5. What is the significance of Christ being at God's right hand? How does this impact you personally?

6. What is your most pressing "do something!" question for God at the moment? How do you sense God answering—or being silent?

Chapter 6: How am I going to get through this?

1. What evidence do you see that we have lost sight of the greater battle? How does this play out in your own life?

2. What kinds of battles do we fight in our daily lives?

3. How did Paul intend for us to use the armor of God passage in Ephesians 6?

4. What are some of the dangers of ignoring the armor? Can you offer a real-life example?

5. In what ways has your view of evil been changed—or your faith strengthened—through reading this book?

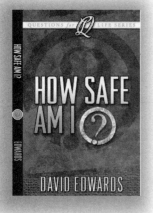
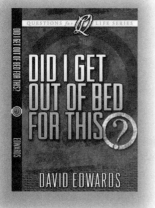

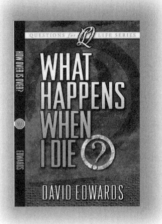

The Word at Work Around the World

A vital part of Cook Communications Ministries is our international outreach, Cook Communications Ministries International (CCMI). Your purchase of this book, and of other books and Christian-growth products from Cook, enables CCMI to provide Bibles and Christian literature to people in more than 150 languages in 65 countries.

Cook Communications Ministries is a not-for-profit, self-supporting organization. Revenues from sales of our books, Bible curricula, and other church and home products not only fund our U.S. ministry, but also fund our CCMI ministry around the world. One hundred percent of donations to CCMI go to our international literature programs.

CCMI reaches out internationally in three ways:

· Our premier International Christian Publishing Institute (ICPI) trains leaders from nationally led publishing houses around the world.

· We provide literature for pastors, evangelists, and Christian workers in their national language.

· We reach people at risk—refugees, AIDS victims, street children, and famine victims—with God's Word.

Word Power, God's Power

Faith Kidz, RiverOak, Honor, Life Journey, Victor, NexGen — every time you purchase a book produced by Cook Communications Ministries, you not only meet a vital personal need in your life or in the life of someone you love, but you're also a part of ministering to José in Colombia, Humberto in Chile, Gousa in India, or Lidiane in Brazil. You help make it possible for a pastor in China, a child in Peru, or a mother in West Africa to enjoy a life-changing book. And because you helped, children and adults around the world are learning God's Word and walking in his ways.

Thank you for your partnership in helping to disciple the world. May God bless you with the power of his Word in your life.

For more information about our international ministries, visit www.ccmi.org.

Additional copies of *Why Is This Happening to Me?*
and other NexGen titles are available
from your local bookseller.
Look for the other books in the Questions for Life series:

Why Is it Taking Me so Long to Be Better?
What Happens When I Die?
Did I Get Out of Bed for This?
Has God Given Up on Me?
How Safe am I?

If you have enjoyed this book,
or if it has had an impact on your life,
we would like to hear from you.

Please contact us at:

NEXGEN BOOKS
Cook Communications Ministries, Dept. 201
4050 Lee Vance View
Colorado Springs, CO 80918
Or visit our Web site: www.cookministries.com

NEXGEN

Building the New Generation of Believers